Quick Lunches & Brunches

A One Foot in the Kitchen Cookbook

Written and Compiled by
CYNDI DUNCAN AND GEORGIE PATRICK

Illustrated by
COLETTE McLAUGHLIN PITCHER

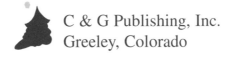

C & G Publishing, Inc.
Greeley, Colorado

Quick Lunches & Brunches

Illustrations by Colette McLaughlin Pitcher
Graphic Design by Gregory Effinger, for
Colorado Independent Graphics, Advertising and Reproduction, www.cigargraphics.com

Nutrition analysis has been calculated on Mastercook II software.

To the best of our knowledge, all information included in this book is correct and complete. The publisher and authors offer no guarantees and disclaim any liability attributed to its use.

Published by C & G Publishing, Inc.
P.O. Box 5199
Greeley, Colorado 80634-0103
For orders and information: (800) 925-3172
www.cgpub.com

To the Georgies and the Cyndis of the world

who look forward to a quiet day

who can finish everyone's sentences except their own

who sleep only 4 hours a night-4 on the couch, 4 in bed

who don't want to find the shoe boxes full of 35 year-old photos

whose "diligently" planned shopping lists never make it to the store

and who have dear friends

this book's for you!

Contents

Introduction   *vi*

Footnotes from Georgie and Cyndi   *vii*

Breads   1

Brunches   25

Lunches   73

Miscellaneous   127

Index   155

Introduction

Change is inevitable. Working on *Quick Lunches & Brunches*, the sixth and final cookbook in our quick meal series, "*One Foot in the Kitchen*", both of us have come to realize that we have experienced that change. Now don't confuse change with capitulation. We still cannot agree on what's quick and easy. But, on that subject, we have agreed to disagree.

On the other hand, Cyndi had a real breakthrough this past year when she discovered fat free hash browns in the freezer section of the grocery store. And, she now claims to have identified 25 different varieties of prepared pie crusts. (Georgie thinks she exaggerates.) Cyndi still wants the world to prepare dishes from their gardens, not realizing yet that the Georgies of this world just don't grow truck farms in their back yards. But, you have to love those sacks of veggies that show up in late spring and early fall. Thank you Cyndis. No matter how many or few shortcuts she discovers, Cyndi is and will always remain an organized and very creative cook.

Georgie, on the other hand, finds herself reading "complicated" recipes in culinary mystery books and actually intending to use some. This doesn't mean she has given up her title of "Queen of Easy" and won't continue to use the deli and her other shortcuts to put meals on the table. She just intends to branch out. (Yeah! Right! Like you have time?) As long as people continue to ask for her delicious creations and don't laugh at how simple they are, she's happy.

One thing neither of us will change is our love of family, good friends and good food. Now, more than any other time in our lives, we have a greater appreciation of life and living. And we intend to live our lives to the fullest.

We hope you have enjoyed using our "*One Foot in the Kitchen*" series as much as we have enjoyed creating it.

Happy Cooking!
Cyndi & Georgie

Footnotes from Cyndi and Georgie

It's been quite a year since we last wrote. For several reasons, we want Quick Lunches & Brunches *to be our best cookbook yet, chocked full of great recipes and much, much more. We think of it as our tribute to the USA in appreciation for all the sacrifices made by families all over the country. We encourage you to find time to cook for your families and friends more often and enjoy QUICK, easy and creative meals.*

Egg substitutes and soy milk can be used in place of real eggs and milk. We advocate using 'light', reduced fat and fat free ingredients when appropriate to reduce calories and fat.

Some of our recipes list a number of ingredients but are still easy to assemble QUICKly. Unlike 3 or 4 ingredient cookbooks, we list seasonings.

The length of baking adds time to meal preparation, but use that time to set the table, wash dishes, read the mail, scratch a lottery ticket or prepare side dishes.

Spice blends, available in stores and at food shows, are a great way to pep up an old recipe. Be creative and unafraid.

Fresh ground pepper and sea salt enhance flavor in recipes. To fill a pepper mill, cut a plastic soda bottle 2-3 inches below the neck, invert and use as a funnel. Works with salt shakers, too.

Microwaving vegetables and fruits in very little water saves nutrients. Using the microwave, blender, food processor and other small appliances saves time.

Oven baking time depends on altitude, humidity and your oven. Watch carefully.

Exercise; who says a few leg lifts done while chopping doesn't help?

Notes:

Breads

DANISH BARS

These QUICK and easy bars offer a delicious layer of flavored cream cheese. They are great served with an egg dish or chili.

2 8-ounce packages cream cheese, softened
3/4 cup sugar
2 tablespoons lemon juice
1 teaspoon vanilla
1 egg yolk
2 8-ounce cans crescent dinner rolls
1 egg white
1 teaspoon water
1/2 cup sliced almonds

Preheat oven to 350°. In mixer bowl, beat cream cheese and sugar until light. Add lemon juice, vanilla and egg yolk. Beat until fluffy. Place 1 can unrolled dough in 9 x 13-inch baking pan. Press perforations to seal. Spread with cream cheese mixture. Top with remaining package of dough pressing perforations to seal. Whisk egg white and water until frothy. Brush on top of dough and sprinkle with almonds. Bake 30 minutes. Cool in pan 20 minutes. Cut into 1 x 2-inch bars. Makes 48.

Per serving: 74 calories; 5.2 fat grams

 For special occasions, spread favorite jam over cream cheese mixture before adding last layer of dough.

CHEDDAR CHEESE BISCUITS

These are similar to the delicious biscuits served at a famous restaurant where we and two other friends meet during the holiday season.

1 1/2 cups flour
1/2 cup yellow cornmeal
2 teaspoons sugar
1 tablespoon baking powder
1/4 teaspoon salt
1/2 cup butter or margarine
1/2 cup cheddar cheese, shredded
1 cup buttermilk

Preheat oven to 450°. In large bowl, combine dry ingredients. With fork or pastry blender, cut in butter until mixture is crumbly. Stir in cheese and milk just until moistened. Drop by heaping tablespoon-fuls onto an ungreased baking sheet. Bake 12-15 minutes or until lightly browned. Makes 12.

Per serving: 175 calories; 9.6 fat grams

 These go well with homemade stew. Make a mock pot pie by placing dough, rolled out on floured surface, over top of a meat casserole and baking.

Breads

DILL AND PARMESAN ROLLS

Plan ahead and allow time for the bread dough to raise. Can't you just imagine these biscuits with a hearty soup?

1 package frozen bread dough rolls
2 tablespoons butter or margarine, melted
1/2 cup Parmesan cheese
1/2 teaspoon dill weed
1/2 teaspoon salt
2 tablespoons butter or margarine, melted
1 tablespoon parsley flakes

Let bread dough thaw and rise as directed on package. Spray or grease well 2 round cake pans. Preheat oven to 375°. Dip each ball into 2 tablespoons melted butter, then dip tops into cheese and arrange in one pan. Arrange remaining balls in other pan. Mix dill weed, salt and 2 tablespoons butter. Brush dill mixture on rolls in second pan. Sprinkle with parsley flakes. Cover; let rise about 20 minutes. Bake 15 minutes or until lightly browned. Makes 36.

Per serving: 112 calories; 2.0 fat grams

 A garlic/olive oil/herb mixture can also be brushed on rolls to accompany an Italian dish.

CARAWAY PUFFS

Georgie's friend, Sally, gave this recipe to her years ago; it has been used for many special occasions.

2 1/3 cups flour
1 package dry yeast
1/4 teaspoon baking soda
1 cup creamy cottage cheese
1/4 cup water
2 tablespoons sugar
1 tablespoon butter
1 teaspoon salt
1 egg
2 teaspoons caraway seeds
2 teaspoons grated onion

In large mixer bowl, combine 1 1/3 cups flour, yeast and soda. Heat cottage cheese, water, sugar, butter and salt to lukewarm. Stir until butter melts. Stir in egg, caraway seed and onion. Add dry ingredients. Beat on low 1/2 minute, then on high 3 minutes. Stir in remaining flour. Place dough in greased bowl, cover and let rise until doubled. Spray or grease muffin pans well. Spoon dough into muffin pans. Cover and let rise 30 minutes. Preheat oven to 400°. Bake 12-15 minutes. Makes 12.

Per serving: 131 calories; 2.0 fat grams

Substitute dill seed for the caraway seeds for a totally different flavor.

Breads

APRICOT BREAD

Apricots bring to mind Cyndi's Aunt Opal who made the very best apricot breads and cobblers from her apricot tree. She didn't write down recipes very often so we are including Georgie's recipe.

2 3-ounce packages cream cheese, softened
1/3 cup sugar
1 tablespoon flour
1 egg
1 teaspoon grated orange peel
1 egg
1/2 cup orange juice
1/2 cup water
1 17-ounce package apricot-nut
    quick bread mix

Preheat oven to 350°. Spray 9 x 5 x 3-inch loaf pan or 2 smaller pans. In large bowl, combine cream cheese, sugar and flour. Beat in first egg and orange peel. Set aside. In large bowl, whisk second egg. Add orange juice and water. Stir in bread mix just until moistened. Turn 2/3 of the batter into loaf pan. Pour cream cheese mixture over top of batter. Spoon on remaining batter. Bake 1 hour. Cool 10 minutes then remove to rack to finish cooling. Wrap in plastic wrap then in foil to store. Serves 12.

Per serving: 239 calories; 8.2 fat grams

 Specific flavors of quick bread mixes are sometimes difficult to find when you want them. Any flavor can be substituted in this recipe.

CRANBERRY BREAD

Use small pans to make gift loaves. Wrap in festive holiday plastic wrap and tie with pretty ribbons.

2 cups flour
1 1/8 cups sugar
1 1/2 teaspoons baking powder
1/2 teaspoon baking soda
1/2 teaspoon salt
1/4 cup shortening or margarine
3/4 cup orange juice
1 tablespoon grated orange peel
1 egg, beaten
1/2 cup nuts, chopped, optional
1/2 cup white raisins, optional
1 1/2 cups cranberries, halved (for
    QUICKer preparation, grind coarsely
    in food processor)

Preheat oven to 325°. Spray 9 x 5 x 3-inch loaf pan and lightly flour. In large bowl, combine dry ingredients. Cut in shortening until mixture resembles coarse corn meal. Add orange juice, peel, egg, nuts, raisins and cranberries. Mix just enough to moisten. Pour into pan. Bake 50-60 minutes. Cool 15 minutes before removing from pan. Refrigerate overnight for easy slicing. Serves 12.

Per serving: 204 calories; 4.9 fat grams

For off-season baking with cranberries, substitute dried cranberries or cherries.

Cranberry Bread is tasty spread with cream cheese or drizzled with butter frosting.

SWEET POPPY SEED BREAD

Thanks to Cyndi's friend, Beverly, for sharing this delicious bread. Bet you can't have just one piece.

3 cups flour
2 1/4 cups sugar
1 1/2 tablespoons poppy seeds
1 1/2 teaspoons salt
1 1/2 teaspoons baking powder
1 1/2 cups vegetable oil
1 1/2 cups lowfat milk
3 eggs
1 1/2 teaspoons almond flavoring
1 1/2 teaspoons butter flavoring

Topping:
1/4 cup orange juice
1/2 teaspoon butter flavoring
3/4 cup sugar
1/2 teaspoon vanilla
1/2 teaspoon almond flavoring

Preheat oven to 350°. Spray 2 medium loaf pans. In large bowl, mix all ingredients together. Pour into pans. Bake 45 minutes. Serves 20-24.

Topping: Heat all ingredients slightly, stirring to dissolve sugar. Pour over warm loaves of bread.

Per serving: 295 calories; 14.9 fat grams

 When cooled, refrigerate for easier slicing.

LEMON BREAD

Georgie's friend, Sally, shared this sticky-topped bread recipe with her many years ago. It's a delicious side to a breakfast or lunch.

1/2 cup shortening
2 tablespoons grated lemon peel
1 cup sugar
2 eggs
1/2 cup milk
1 1/2 cups flour
1 teaspoon baking powder
1/2 teaspoon salt

Glaze:
1/4 cup sugar
Juice from 1 lemon

Preheat oven to 350°. Spray large loaf pan. In large bowl, cream together shortening, lemon peel, sugar and eggs. Stir in milk. Add flour, baking powder and salt. Pour into pan. Bake 45-50 minutes. While hot, spoon glaze over top. Serves 12.

Glaze: Combine sugar and lemon juice. Pour over hot loaves of bread.

Per serving: 230 calories; 9.7 fat grams

Foot Note To freeze, wrap tightly with plastic wrap and place in zippered freezer bag. Insert small crumpled, slightly dampened piece of paper toweling to absorb freezer taste. Press excess air out of bag as zipping. Store up to 6 months.

Breads

POPPY SEED BREAD

Georgie's favorite muffin is poppy seed. She often orders poppy seed dressing and now she offers you her favorite poppy seed bread recipe.

1 cup sugar
2 eggs
1 cup evaporated milk
1 cup oil
2 cups flour
2 teaspoons baking powder
1/4 teaspoon salt
1 teaspoon vanilla
1/4 cup poppy seeds

Preheat oven to 350°. Spray large loaf pan. In large bowl, combine sugar, eggs, milk and oil. Beat on medium until well blended. Sift together flour, baking powder and salt. Add flour mixture to egg mixture. Mix on low. Add vanilla and poppy seeds. Mix about 2 minutes. Pour into loaf pan. Bake 1 hour or until tester inserted in middle comes out clean. Serves 12-14.

Per serving: 305 calories; 18.8 fat grams

> **Foot Note** A serving idea: spread 1 slice chilled bread with butter and jelly or cream cheese and marmalade; top with another slice. Cut in fourths and spear one of the pieces with a long cocktail pick. Next spear grape, strawberry, banana slice or other favorite piece of fruit. Repeat 2 or 3 more times and serve as a 'kabob' side to a salad, soup or brunch dish.

PUMPKIN BREAD

This has to be almost everyone's favorite, no matter what time of year it is.

3 cups sugar
3 1/2 cups flour
2 teaspoons baking soda
1 teaspoon cinnamon
1 teaspoon nutmeg
1/2 teaspoon salt
4 eggs
1 cup vegetable oil
2/3 cup water
2 cups pumpkin

Preheat oven to 350°. Spray two 9 x 5 x 3-inch loaf pans. In large bowl, combine dry ingredients; make well in center and set aside. In large bowl, beat eggs until creamy. Beat in oil, water and pumpkin. Pour into dry ingredients and mix well. Divide batter evenly into pans. Bake 45-55 minutes. Serves 24.

Per serving: 262 calories; 10.1 fat grams

Foot Notes

Try baking pumpkin bread in generously sprayed 3 1-pound coffee cans. These nice round loaves help perk up your presentation.

Frost with cream cheese frosting.
Cream Cheese Frosting
1 3-ounce package cream cheese
1/2 cup butter or margarine, softened
1 teaspoon vanilla or 1/2 teaspoon almond extract
2 cups powdered sugar
Beat all ingredients together until smooth.

Breads

PINEAPPLE ZUCCHINI BREAD

The pineapple and zucchini in this spicy bread keep it nice and moist.

3 eggs, slightly beaten
2 cups sugar
1 cup oil
2 teaspoons vanilla
2 cups, zucchini, unpeeled, shredded
1 16-ounce can crushed pineapple,
   well drained
3 1/4 cups flour
2 teaspoons baking soda
1/2 teaspoon baking powder
1 1/2 teaspoons cinnamon
3/4 teaspoon nutmeg
1/2 teaspoon salt
1 cup raisins or chopped dates, optional
1 cup walnuts or pecans, chopped

Preheat oven to 350°. Spray 2 9 x 5 x 3-inch loaf pans. In large bowl, beat eggs, sugar, oil and vanilla. Add remaining ingredients and mix well, but do not over mix. Fill loaf pans about 2/3 full. Bake 45-50 minutes or until tester pick inserted into center comes out clean. Let set 5 minutes before removing from pan. Serves 24.

Per serving: 254 calories; 10.6 fat grams

Foot Notes

Quick breads fall because there is too much baking powder in the recipe. In that case, next time you make it, increase the baking soda to balance acid and alkali. Before changing a recipe make sure you have measured correctly.

For a zesty orange flavor, add 2 tablespoons shredded orange peel and 1/4 cup orange juice concentrate.

SPICED PECAN COFFEE CAKE

The spiced nutty center makes this coffee cake an awesome addition to any brunch or lunch

1 cup butter or margarine
2 cups sugar
2 eggs
1 cup light sour cream
1/2 teaspoon vanilla
1/2 teaspoon almond extract
2 cups flour, sifted
1 teaspoon baking powder
1/4 teaspoon salt
4 teaspoons sugar
1 cup pecans, chopped
1 teaspoon cinnamon

Preheat oven to 350°. Spray and flour bundt cake pan. In large mixing bowl, cream butter and sugar. Add eggs, one at a time, beating after each addition. Add sour cream, vanilla and almond extract; beat well. In separate bowl, combine flour, baking powder and salt. Add to butter mixture and beat. In separate bowl, combine sugar, pecans, and cinnamon for filling. Spoon 1/3 of batter in pan. Sprinkle with 3/4 of filling mixture. Spoon in rest of batter and sprinkle with remainder of filling. Bake 1 hour. Cool slightly. Remove cake to rack to cool. Serves 16.

Per serving: 321 calories; 17.5 fat grams

For a streusel effect, make a zig-zag pattern with a knife through the batter after sprinkling on filling layer.

CORNMEAL STREUSEL COFFEE CAKE

Cornmeal never tasted so good.

4 teaspoons instant coffee
1/2 cup lowfat milk
2 eggs, beaten
1/4 cup butter or margarine, melted
1 cup flour
2/3 cup brown sugar, firmly packed
1/2 cup cornmeal
1 1/2 teaspoons baking powder
1/4 teaspoon baking soda
1/2 teaspoon salt

Streusel Topping:
2 tablespoons cornmeal
2 tablespoons brown sugar, firmly packed
1 tablespoon butter or margarine melted
1/3 cup sliced almonds

Preheat oven to 375°. Spray 8 x 8-inch baking dish. In small bowl, dissolve coffee in milk. Add eggs and butter; mix well. In large bowl, combine dry ingredients. Stir in milk mixture just until moistened. Pour into baking dish. Sprinkle with streusel topping. Bake 20-25 minutes. Test for doneness. Cool slightly. Serves 9.

Streusel Topping:
In large bowl, combine cornmeal, brown sugar and butter mixing until crumbly. Add nuts. Sprinkle over batter.

Per serving: 241 calories; 10.5 fat grams

For QUICK way to soften brown sugar, place piece of apple in bag and microwave 10 seconds. Let set 1 minute. Repeat at short intervals if first try did not work. Do not melt brown sugar.

GEORGIE'S MONKEY BREAD

This is a Christmas morning staple at the Patrick home. Can't you just smell it?

1/2 cup sugar
1 teaspoon cinnamon
2 cans big butter-flavored biscuits
1/2 cup pecans, coarsely chopped, optional
1 1/4 cups brown sugar
1/2 cup butter or margarine, melted

Preheat oven to 375°. Heavily butter bundt pan. Mix sugar and cinnamon in pie pan. Cut each biscuit into 8ths. Roll each piece in cinnamon mixture. Place 1/2 of pieces in bundt pan. If using nuts, spread 1/2 over biscuits. In small pan, combine brown sugar and butter. Stir over medium heat until blended; bring to boil. Pour half of mixture over biscuit pieces. Repeat procedure. Bake 30-40 minutes. Serves 8-12.

Per serving: 409 calories; 19.6 fat grams

Foot Notes

As a 'wreath' holiday centerpiece, decorate hole with sprigs of holly and put cranberries around the bottom.

As a fun 'pizza', place biscuit pieces on round baking sheet and top with sugar mixture. While still warm, cut wheel with pizza cutter.

ANGEL BUNS

Georgie's Aunt Sallie, a good cook herself, makes these delicious and easy buns for breakfast and/or lunch.

1 package quick acting dry yeast
1 tablespoon sugar
1/4 cup warm water (105-115°)
2 cups baking mix
1/4 cup milk

In medium bowl, dissolve yeast and sugar in warm water. Stir in baking mix and milk until dough forms (do not over mix). On cutting board dusted with biscuit mix or flour, knead bread 10 times. Roll out 1/2-inch thick. Cut with 2-inch biscuit cutter or glass dipped in biscuit mix or flour. Place on ungreased baking sheet. Let rise in warm place 30 minutes. Heat oven to 425°. Bake 6-8 minutes. (High Altitude: Let rise 20 minutes. Bake 450° about 5 minutes.) Serves 10.

Per serving: 108 calories; 3.5 fat grams

If there should be any of these Angel Buns left over, use in bread pudding or cut into cubes, toss with olive oil and your favorite herb mixture, microwave until dry and lightly browned, and use as croutons.

GERMAN DONUTS

This recipe was given to Cyndi by a friend in Brush, CO. Called 'Graebble' (one of many spellings) in the German community; they are deep fried and definitely a splurge.

2 eggs
3/4 cup evaporated milk
3/4 cup water
3 tablespoons sugar
3 1/2 cups flour
2 teaspoons baking powder
Pinch of allspice
1 teaspoon salt
2 tablespoons butter or margarine, melted
2 cups oil
1 cup sugar
1 teaspoon vanilla

In large bowl, beat eggs until light. Add milk, water and 3 tablespoons sugar. Sift flour, baking powder, allspice and salt. Add to egg mixture; mix with spoon. Add melted butter; mix. Let set at room temperature for 2 or 3 hours, or in refrigerator over-night. Heat oil to 400°. Roll out dough on floured surface 1/4-inch thick. Cut into 1 x 4-inch strips with pizza cutter. Cut slit lengthwise in center and twist each piece. Fry in hot oil turning until lightly browned. Remove and drain on paper towel. Mix 1 cup sugar and vanilla in paper bag. Toss warm donuts in sugar mixture. Remove and cool on rack. Serves 15-20.

Per serving: 232 calories; 13.4 fat grams

Foot Notes An electric skillet works well when heating oil. Using lard or shortening will make donuts greasier.

This dough can be frozen. Leave at room temperature the night before using.

RHUBARB-ORANGE MUFFINS

Rhubarb is usually a spring treat, but use frozen rhubarb for year long baking.

2 cups flour
3/4 cup sugar
1 1/2 teaspoons baking powder
1/2 teaspoon baking soda
3/4 cup pecans, chopped
1 1/4 cups rhubarb, chopped
1/4 cup oil
3/4 cup orange juice
1 egg
2 teaspoons grated orange peel

Preheat oven to 400°. Spray muffin tin. In small bowl, combine dry ingredients. Toss pecans and rhubarb into flour mixture to coat. In small bowl, whisk egg. Stir in oil, orange juice and peel. Mix with dry ingredients until just moistened. Fill muffin cups 2/3 full. Bake 20-25 minutes. Serves 12.

Per serving: 203 calories; 7.6 fat grams

Over mixing muffins can cause tunnels and a more cake-like texture.

If offering a variety of muffins, use mini muffin tins, giving your guests a chance to try several flavors. (Remember to reduce baking time.)

BLUEBERRY CRUMB MUFFINS

Blueberry muffins go with absolutely everything; breakfast, lunch or dinner. (Well, maybe not; Georgie doesn't think she'd like them with Italian or Mexican food.)

1/4 cup butter or margarine, softened
1/3 cup sugar
1 egg
2 1/3 cups flour
4 teaspoons baking powder
1/2 teaspoon salt
1 cup milk
1 teaspoon vanilla
1 1/2 cups fresh or frozen blueberries.
   rinsed

<u>**Topping**</u>:
1/2 cup sugar
1/3 cup flour
1/2 teaspoon cinnamon
1/4 cup butter or margarine, softened

Preheat oven to 375°. Spray muffin tins. In large mixer bowl, cream 1/4 cup butter and 1/3 cup sugar until light and fluffy. Beat in egg. In medium bowl, combine flour, baking powder and salt; add alternately with milk, mixing just until moistened. Stir in vanilla and blueberries. Fill muffin cups 2/3 full. Sprinkle topping on top of batter. Bake 25-30 minutes. Serves 18.

Topping: In small bowl, mix sugar, flour and cinnamon. Cut in butter until crumbly. Sprinkle over muffin batter.

Per serving: 167 calories; 6.0 fat grams

If using paper baking cups, spray them with nonstick cooking spray to keep from clinging to muffin.

BREADSTICKS

These simple-to-make, bakery-fresh treats offer a variety of coatings.

1 package refrigerated breadstick dough

Coatings:

Spread dough with dijon mustard. Layer breadstick with snipped prosciutto and Parmesan cheese.

Brush on favorite pesto sauce and press pine nuts or sunflower seeds into dough.

Dip in olive oil, then in coarsely chopped thyme or parsley. Sprinkle with garlic salt.

Dip in Italian salad dressing, then Parmesan cheese. Sprinkle with white cheddar cheese.

Press taco meat into bread dough, twist and brush with salsa juice.

Preheat oven to 400°. Spray large baking sheet. Separate dough into strips. Fill each one with desired fillings. Twist the breadstick dough around fillings. Don't worry if the breadsticks aren't perfect or if some of the filling falls out. Place breadsticks on baking sheet. Bake 5 minutes until lightly browned. Serves 12.

Per serving: 110 calories; 4.9 fat grams
(approximate; varies with each filling)

Sweet Breadsticks:

Coat with honey, sprinkle with cinnamon. Press in granola and chocolate candy pieces. Brush with melted butter.

Brush dough with butter and sprinkle with cinnamon sugar

Spread your favorite pie filling on breadstick, twist and bake.

DILLY BREAD

Cyndi's aunt gave this recipe to her when she was just a young girl. It is often requested for family dinners. Even though it is a yeast bread, it is easy; just start preparation early.

1 packet dry yeast
1/4 cup warm water
1 cup cottage cheese, heated to lukewarm
2 tablespoons sugar
1 tablespoon onion, minced
1 tablespoon butter or margarine
2 teaspoons dill seed
1/2 teaspoon salt
1/4 teaspoon baking soda
1 egg
2 1/4 cups flour

Spray deep pie dish. Soften yeast in warm water. In large bowl, combine remaining ingredients and yeast mixture. Stir just until moistened. Place in baking dish. Cover and let rise in warm place until light and doubled in size, about 50 minutes. Preheat oven to 400°. Bake 15-20 minutes. Brush top with melted butter. Serves 8.

Per serving: 192 calories; 3.0 fat grams

 If you are caught without dill seed, you can use dill weed. The flavor is different but still very good.

FRENCH CHEESE BREAD

Be creative in your toppings for this bread.

1 loaf sour dough French bread, sliced
    lengthwise
1 cup butter or margarine, softened
2 cups sharp cheddar cheese, shredded
1/4 cup Romano cheese, grated
1 teaspoon Worcestershire sauce
1/4 teaspoon garlic powder
1/2 teaspoon paprika
1 teaspoon poppy seeds

Set oven to broil. Place bread on large baking sheet. In large bowl, combine remaining ingredients; mix well. Spread on both halves of the bread. Toast under broiler 5 minutes. Slice diagonally. Serves 16.

Per serving: 244 calories; 17.5 fat grams

Romano cheese is not a good eating cheese like cheddar, but is robust in flavor when melted on breads and in pasta dishes.

TOMATO-BASIL FOCACCIA

This recipe from Georgie is written on a tan napkin. We tried this in a little shop in Santa Fe when attending a book fair.

1 tablespoon cornmeal
12-inch Italian pizza crust
2 tablespoons olive oil
2 tomatoes, chopped
1 red onion, thinly sliced
1/2 cup fresh basil, chopped
1 teaspoon poppy seeds
1 teaspoon sesame seeds
1/2 teaspoon garlic salt
4 ounces Swiss cheese, shredded

Set oven to broil. Sprinkle 12-inch pizza pan with cornmeal. Place pizza crust in pan. In large bowl, combine olive oil, tomatoes, onion, basil, poppy seeds, sesame seeds and garlic salt. Spoon onto bread. Top with cheese. Broil 5-10 minutes or until cheese is melted. Serves 8.

Per serving: 216 calories; 12.4 fat grams

Focaccia bread can be 'loaded' up with a variety of ingredients, so experiment with those you love to eat. Focaccia is a great bread to serve with salads and soups.

Notes:

Brunches

BASIC CREPES

The French word 'crepes' rhymes with 'preps', or also pronounced 'crepes' that rhymes with 'drapes', are light wraparounds for a variety of sweet, vegetable, cheese or meat fillings.

Basic Crepes
1 cup flour
1/4 teaspoon salt
2 eggs
3/4 cup milk or cream
1/2 cup water
3 tablespoons oil or butter, melted

Dessert Crepes - Add to the basic recipe
2 tablespoons sugar

Light Crepes - Substitutions in basic recipe
Use skim milk
Use only 1 egg
Omit oil or butter

Easy substitutions and/ or additions
Use whole wheat flour
Add a tablespoon or two of cornmeal
Add 1/2 cup sour cream
Use chocolate milk

In large bowl, beat all ingredients until well blended. Lightly grease and heat a 6-inch skillet or large griddle. Remove from heat and spoon in 2 tablespoons batter. Tilt skillet to spread batter evenly. Return to heat and brown on one side only. Turn out onto paper toweling. Repeat with rest of batter. Spray skillet occasionally. Makes 18.

Per serving:
Basic Crepes: *59 calories; 3.2 fat grams*
Dessert Crepes: *64 calories; 3.2 fat grams*
Light Crepes: *38 calories; 0.3 fat grams*

 Make crepes a day, a week or months ahead because crepes freeze well. Separate with two layers of waxed paper, stack in a zipping bag and store in a plastic or glass container. Thaw at room temperature.

CHICKEN DIVAN CREPES

Make your favorite Divan into a rolled delicacy.

1 10-ounce can cream of chicken soup
1/2 cup light mayonnaise
1 teaspoon Worcestershire sauce
1 teaspoon curry powder
1 tablespoon lemon juice
2 cups chicken breast, diced or shredded
1 10-ounce package frozen chopped
　　broccoli, drained
20 crepes
1/4 cup milk or dry white wine
1/2 cup cheddar cheese, shredded

Make crepes from recipe on page 26. Preheat oven to 375°. Spray 9 x 13-inch casserole dish. In large bowl, combine soup, mayonnaise, Worcestershire sauce, curry powder and lemon juice. Mix well. Reserve 1 cup for topping. Add chicken and broccoli to soup mixture. Fill crepes with mixture. Roll and place in casserole dish. To the reserved topping mixture add 1/4 cup milk. Drizzle sauce over crepes. Sprinkle with cheese. Bake 25-30 minutes. Serves 10.

Per serving: 246 calories; 13.8 fat grams

Substitute ham and asparagus for chicken and broccoli. Omit the curry powder and add 1 teaspoon dry mustard to sauce mixture. Instead of chopping the ham, roll asparagus inside thin ham slices. Spread sauce on crepe and roll with ham roll inside. Place in dish and drizzle remaining sauce on top.

Crepes

TURKEY AND CRANBERRY CREPES

Leftover Thanksgiving turkey (or deli-fresh) and cranberry sauce are enhanced by a secret ingredient in this recipe.

2 cups cooked turkey, chopped
1/2 cup unpeeled cucumber, finely chopped
1/2 cup onion, finely chopped
1/2 cup light mayonnaise or salad dressing
20 crepes
1 teaspoon cornstarch
1 16-ounce can whole cranberry sauce

Preheat oven to 375°. Spray 9 x 13-inch baking dish. In large bowl, combine turkey, cucumber, onion and mayonnaise. Spread 3 tablespoons filling onto unbrowned side of crepe, leaving 1/4-inch rim around edge. Roll up crepe. Place seam down in baking dish. Repeat. Cover with foil and bake 20 minutes. In the meantime, heat cornstarch and cranberry sauce until thickened and bubbly. Remove crepes to dinner plates. Spoon sauce over each serving. Serves 10.

Per serving: 234 calories; 8.1 fat grams

Leftover cranberry salad can be used in place of canned cranberry sauce.

Fresh cranberries can be stored in refrigerator for several months. They can be frozen for years without diminishing quality. When thawed, cranberries will become soft and need to be used immediately.

ARTICHOKE AND SPINACH CREPES

These crepes can be used for hors d'oeuvres or as a main dish filled with your favorite beef, chicken, fish or vegetable mixture.

6 eggs
1/3 cup water
1 10-ounce jar artichokes, chopped
1 10-ounce package chopped frozen
    spinach, thawed, and well drained
1/2 cup Swiss cheese, shredded
12 crepes
1/4 cup black olives, sliced
1/4 cup green onion, sliced

Preheat oven to 375°. Spray muffin tin. In large bowl, beat eggs and water until mixed well. Stir in artichokes, spinach and cheese. Press crepes in muffin cups. Spoon egg mixture evenly into cups. Bake 30 minutes. Let set 2-3 minutes to firm up. Remove to serving plate and garnish each with black olives and green onion. Serves 6.

Per serving: 260 calories; 14.1 fat grams

Foot Notes

Using water in beaten egg dishes will make eggs cook up fluffier. Adding milk makes a denser product.

Crepe Cups
Preheat oven to 375°. Generously grease outside of custard cup; turn upside down on baking sheet. Place crepe, browned side up, over cup and press lightly to shape. Bake 20 minutes or until crisp. Cool and carefully remove from cup. Fill with salads or cool desserts.

SPINACH CREPES

This recipe came to Cyndi and Georgie through Newcomers Club Recipe Group when they first moved to Greeley.

1 large onion, chopped
1 clove garlic, finely chopped
1 tablespoon oil
2 10-ounce packages frozen chopped
    spinach, cooked and drained
2 cups partially skimmed milk ricotta
    cheese
1 1/2 cups mozzarella cheese, divided (sep-
    arate 1/2 cup for topping)
1/2 cup Parmesan cheese
3 eggs, beaten
1 tablespoon lemon juice
1/2 teaspoon salt
1/8 teaspoon nutmeg
1/4 teaspoon pepper
24 crepes

Preheat oven to 375°. Spray covered casserole dish. In large skillet, sauté onion and garlic in oil until tender, but not browned. Remove from heat. Add spinach to onion mixture, along with next 8 ingredients. Mix well. Spoon filling into center of crepes and roll up. Place in casserole dish seam side down. Bake 20 minutes. Remove cover and sprinkle with remaining 1/2 cup cheese. Bake 5 minutes longer. Serves 12.

Per serving: 275 calories; 16.5 fat grams

 If desired, top with a favorite sauce.
Hollandaise sauce (page 62)
Bearnaise Sauce
    3/4 teaspoon onion, grated
    1 teaspoon minced parsley
    2 teaspoons tarragon vinegar
    1/4 teaspoon tarragon
To Hollandaise sauce add remaining ingredients. Can be made ahead and covered. Keep warm until ready to serve by placing over hot, not boiling, water.

SEAFOOD CREPES

Also acquired from a Newcomers Recipe Club friend.

4 tablespoons butter or margarine
4 tablespoons flour
1 2/3 cups half & half
1 teaspoon salt (less, if desired)
Pepper to taste
1/4 teaspoon paprika
1/3 cup white wine
2 cups shrimp, lobster, crab, scallops,
    salmon or a good white fish
12 crepes

In large pan, melt butter; stir in flour. Gradually add half & half. Cook over low heat, stirring constantly, until thick. Add salt, pepper and paprika. Cook over low heat 2 minutes, stirring often. Do not boil. Remove from heat. Gradually stir in wine. Add seafood. Reheat to serving temperature. Spoon 4 tablespoons mixture in center of crepe. Fold ends in toward center. Roll up and place on individual plates. Serve immediately. Serves 6.

Per serving: 336 calories; 22.3 fat grams
(varies with type of seafood used)

 Again, these can be topped with sauce.
Cheese Sauce:
1 tablespoon each butter and flour
Salt and pepper to taste
1/4 teaspoon dry mustard
1 cup milk
1/2 cup sharp American cheese, cut up
Heat first 6 ingredients over low heat until smooth and bubbly. Remove from heat. Add cheese, stirring until melted.

HAM AND CHEESE CREPES

Calories and fat grams can be reduced in this recipe by using milk in place of cream and less cheese.

1/2 cup butter or margarine
1/2 cup flour
2 cups light cream
2 cups cooked extra lean ham, cubed
1 cup Swiss cheese, cubed
2 4-ounce cans mushrooms in liquid
1/2 teaspoon salt
1/2 teaspoon pepper
24 crepes
Sauce (recipe below)

Preheat oven to 350°. Spray 9 x 13-inch baking dish. In medium saucepan, melt butter over medium heat. Remove from heat and add flour. Gradually add cream, stirring often until smooth. Cook, stirring constantly until thickened. Add ham, cheese, mushrooms, salt and pepper. Stir until cheese is almost melted. Spoon filling into center of each crepe. Roll and place seam side down in baking dish. Cover crepes with sauce. Bake, covered, 45 minutes. Remove cover and broil 3-5 minutes. Serves 12.

Cheese Sauce

2 tablespoons butter or margarine
2 tablespoons flour
2 cups light cream
2 tablespoon wine, sherry or apple cider
1/2 cup Swiss cheese, shredded
Dash salt and pepper

Cheese Sauce

In medium pan, blend butter and flour. Gradually add cream, stirring until thickened. Stir in wine, cheese, salt and pepper until cheese is melted. Thin sauce with water if too thick.

Per serving: 543 calories; 41.7 fat grams

Crepes

BAKED BLINTZES

This is a delicious, not-too-sweet side dish to eggs. Top with favorite fruit compotes, or serve plain and offer jam or sour cream and cinnamon sugar.

1 egg, beaten
1 1/2 cups dry cottage cheese
2 tablespoons sugar
1/2 teaspoon vanilla
Dash ground cinnamon
12 crepes
2 tablespoons butter or margarine
1 15-ounce can cherry (or any flavor) pie
    filling, heated
1/2 cup sour cream, optional

In large bowl, beat together egg, cottage cheese, sugar, vanilla and cinnamon until almost smooth. Spoon cheese mixture in center of unbrowned side of each crepe. Fold over opposite edges to overlap over filling like an envelope. In a large skillet, melt butter and sauté crepe 'envelopes' on both sides until heated through. Remove to warm plate, dollop with warm pie filling and spoonfuls of sour cream. Serves 6.

Per serving: 320 calories; 15.2 fat grams

For a QUICKer way to heat, brush crepe 'envelopes' with butter, place in a large baking dish and heat in a 250° oven until warm. Remove to individual serving plates.

BASIC OMELET

Omelets can be filled with many flavors. The Duncan favorite is a mixture of fresh vegetables from their garden. We list a few combinations for good fillers, but you can create your own, too.

8 eggs
1/2 cup water
1/2 teaspoon salt
1/4 teaspoon pepper
1/2 teaspoon oregano
1 tablespoon butter or margarine
1/2 cup cheese, shredded

Suggested Fillings:
Sautéed combination of vegetables (onion,
    zucchini, peppers, tomatoes)
Ham and broccoli
Chicken and asparagus
Shrimp
Bacon and tomato
Crab and spinach

In medium bowl, beat eggs until mixed well. Add water, salt, pepper and oregano. Melt butter in large sprayed skillet. Pour egg mixture into heated skillet. As eggs set, gently lift edges with heat proof spatula, allowing uncooked portion to flow underneath. Tilt pan slightly in each direction. When eggs are set, but still moist, place filling ingredients on one side of omelet. Carefully fold in half. Cover and let stand until eggs are completely set (and, if you added cheese, until it's melted). Serves 4.

Per serving: 206 calories; 15.8 grams

> **Foot Notes** To make individual omelets, heat oven to 300°. In two small sprayed skillets, heat 3/4 teaspoon butter. Pour 1/2-3/4 cup egg mixture into skillets and proceed as instructed above. Keep warm in oven while repeating the process.
>
> Egg substitutes can be used in these recipes. They are 99% eggs with no fat, no cholesterol, and less than half the calories.

Omelets

SPINACH AND TOMATO SALSA OMELET

Creativity is the key to fixing great egg dishes. Look in your garden, refrigerator and/or pantry for inspiration.

1 onion, chopped
3-4 tomatoes, cut up
2 cups fresh spinach, cut up
2 tablespoons olive oil
8 eggs
1/3 cup water
3/4 teaspoon oregano
Salt and pepper to taste
1 3-ounce light cream cheese, cubed
3/4 cup Monterey Jack cheese

In small skillet, sauté onion, tomatoes and spinach 5 minutes in olive oil. Keep warm while preparing eggs. In large bowl, beat together eggs, water, oregano, salt and pepper. Stir in cream cheese. Pour egg mixture into sprayed large skillet or omelet pan. Cook over medium heat, loosening periodically and tipping pan to allow liquid to run underneath. When still creamy on top, add cheese to half of omelet. Fold over carefully with heat resistant spatulas. Reduce heat. Slide pan back and forth over heat several times to melt cheese and finish cooking process. Divide into serving pieces. To serve, spread 2-3 tablespoons salsa on plate before placing omelet, then top with 3-4 more tablespoons salsa. Serves 4.

Per serving: 344 calories; 25.8 fat grams

 Add zucchini to the tomato mixture when it is plentiful.

SALMON OMELET WITH CUCUMBER SAUCE

Sounds odd, but it is very delicious. Use this cucumber sauce in other recipes.

1/2 cup light sour cream
1/2 cup peeled cucumber, chopped
1 tablespoon green onions with tops,
    minced
1/2 teaspoon dill weed
1 7-ounce can salmon with liquid
8 eggs
1/2 cup water
1/4 teaspoon salt
Pepper to taste
1/4 cup butter or margarine
Fresh dill, optional

In small bowl, mix sour cream, cucumber, onions and dill together. Refrigerate while preparing omelet. In small pan, flake and heat salmon and its liquid. In large bowl, beat eggs, water, salt and pepper. Make individual omelets by using small skillet. Melt 1 tablespoon butter in skillet. When hot, pour 1/2 cup egg mixture into skillet. Tilt pan and lift edges to allow egg mixture to flow underneath. While top is moist and creamy, fill omelet with 1/4 cup drained salmon. Fold omelet in half with spatula. Place on serving plate and keep warm while making other omelets. To serve, top each omelet with 1/4 cup chilled cucumber sauce Garnish with fresh dill. Serves 4.

Per serving: 296 calories; 22.2 fat grams

 This can be made as one large omelet and divided into 4 servings before adding sauce.

ITALIAN HARVEST OMELET

Cyndi loves summer and harvesting her huge garden. Even if you don't have a garden, visit your local farmers' market or nearest roadside stand for fresh produce.

2 tablespoons olive oil
1 cup onion, chopped
1 clove garlic, chopped
1 cup zucchini, cubed
1 cup green peppers, or combination of red, green and yellow peppers, sliced
3/4 cup fresh mushrooms, sliced
1/4 cup corn kernels cut from leftover ear of corn
1 15-ounce can Italian tomato sauce, or 3 fresh tomatoes and 1 8-ounce can Italian tomato sauce
6 eggs
1/4 teaspoon salt
1/4 cup lowfat milk
1/4 cup Parmesan cheese
1/4 teaspoon pepper
1 teaspoon oregano
2 tablespoons butter or margarine
1 cup mozzarella cheese

In medium saucepan, heat oil and sauté vegetables 5 minutes. Add tomato sauce and keep warm while preparing omelet. In large mixing bowl, beat eggs until creamy. Add salt, milk, Parmesan cheese, pepper and oregano. Mix well. Preheat oven to 350°. In 10-inch ovenproof skillet, melt butter and add egg mixture. Over medium-low heat cook 8 minutes, lifting edges to allow uncooked portion to flow underneath. Place in oven 3-4 minutes to finish cooking. Remove and sprinkle with cheese. Fold over. Place on serving plate and top with tomato sauce mixture. Serves 4.

Per serving: 389 calories; 28.1 fat grams

Foot Note

For a Mexican flavor, substitute chile peppers and/or jalapeños for the green peppers and Mexican tomato sauce for Italian tomato sauce. The oregano enhances Mexican food flavor, but also add 1/2 teaspoon chili powder and 1/2 teaspoon cumin.

EGG & SAUSAGE QUICHE

The use of both hard-cooked and beaten eggs makes this hearty quiche unique. Using lowfat cheese, egg substitute and lowfat milk will make it lighter.

Pastry for 1-crust 9-inch pie
8 ounces bulk pork sausage
4 hard-cooked eggs, chopped
1 cup Swiss cheese, shredded
1 cup cheddar cheese, shredded
3 eggs, beaten
1 1/4 cups light cream or milk
1/2 teaspoon salt
1/8 teaspoon pepper

Preheat oven to 350°. Line pie plate with pastry. Flute edges. *Do not prick.* Bake 7 minutes. In skillet, cook sausage; drain well. Spread hard-cooked eggs in bottom of pie shell; top with sausage and cheeses. Combine beaten eggs, cream, salt and pepper. Pour over all. Bake 30-45 minutes or until set. Let stand 10 minutes before serving. Serves 8.

Per serving: 404 calories; 30.7 fat grams

Baking the pie crust before putting ingredients into it helps prevent it from getting soggy when filling is added.

Freshness counts when choosing eggs. Be sure to check 'sell by' date on carton. It is preferable to store eggs in the carton in the refrigerator to prevent absorbing odors from other foods and losing moisture.

HAM AND VEGETABLE QUICHE

Crisp fried bacon or Canadian bacon are good in this quiche, too.

Pastry for 2 10-inch pies
1 cup broccoli, finely chopped
1/2 cup carrots, finely chopped
1/2 cup onions, finely chopped
1/2 cup green pepper, finely chopped
2 tablespoons butter or chicken broth
1 1/3 cups ham, finely chopped
2 cups cheddar cheese, shredded
6 eggs, beaten
2 cups milk
1/2 teaspoon salt

Preheat oven to 425°. Line pie plates with pastry. Prick bottom and sides lightly with fork. Bake 5 minutes. Cool. In large skillet, sauté vegetables in butter or broth. Mix in ham and 1 cup cheese. Divide equally between pastry shells. In large bowl, beat eggs, milk and salt well. Pour over vegetables in pastry shells. Top with remaining 1 cup cheese. Bake on lowest shelf in oven 40-45 minutes or until set. Let stand 10 minutes before serving. Serves 12.

Per serving: 312 calories; 20.8 fat grams

If using frozen pastry, use a 10-inch deep dish pie shell. Let thaw about 20 minutes before pricking.

Overbaking quiche is a common mistake. When baking time is up, quiche is still a little shaky in the middle. Allow it to stand 10 minutes to set up.

Quiches

SWISS QUICHE

This may be the most common of quiches. It can go crustless.

Pastry for 2 pie crusts
1 cup Swiss cheese, shredded
1 10-ounce package frozen chopped
    spinach, thawed and drained well
1 cup heavy cream
1 cup milk
3 eggs
1 medium onion, chopped
1/4 cup flour
3/4 teaspoon salt
1/4 teaspoon pepper
1/4 teaspoon nutmeg

Preheat oven to 400°. Line pastry in 2 9-inch pie plates. Spread cheese and spinach in unbaked pie shells. Whirl rest of ingredients in blender. Pour over cheese and spinach. Bake 35-40 minutes. Serves 12.

Per serving: 284 calories; 19.9 fat grams

Foot Note To make this quiche lighter, use half & half cream and lowfat milk. Better yet, use egg substitute with light milk. The texture will not be quite as creamy, but the flavor is not altered.

BACON AND MUSHROOM QUICHE

This quiche is a Georgie favorite to prepare for bridge luncheons and family brunches. To save a few calories, make it crustless and reduce amount of bacon used.

Pastry for 1 pie crust
1 cup crisp fried bacon, crumbled
1/4 cup onion flakes or 1 onion, chopped
    and sautéed
1 4-ounce can mushrooms, drained
1 cup Swiss cheese, shredded
1 tablespoon flour
3 eggs
1 cup light cream
1 teaspoon salt
1/2 teaspoon pepper

Preheat oven to 375°. Line pie plate with pastry. Spread bacon, onion and mushrooms in bottom of pie shell. In medium bowl, toss cheese and flour. Spread in pie shell. In large bowl, beat eggs, cream, salt and pepper together. Pour into pie shell. Bake 40-45 minutes or until inserted knife in center comes out clean. Serves 6.

Per serving: 556 calories; 42.7 fat grams

 Use deep dish pie plates to prevent quiches from running over in the oven.

Quiches

MUSHROOM CRUST QUICHE

Enjoy a light quiche with an unusual crust.

1/2 pound mushrooms, coarsely chopped
5 tablespoons butter or margarine
14 saltine crackers, finely crushed (fat-free
    ones are good)
3/4 cup green onions, chopped
2 cups Monterey Jack cheese, shredded
1 cup cottage cheese
3 eggs
1/4 teaspoon cayenne pepper
1/4 teaspoon paprika

Preheat oven to 350°. Spray 9-inch pie pan well. In medium skillet, over medium heat, sauté the mushrooms in 3 tablespoons of butter until limp. Stir in crackers. Press mushroom mixture evenly over bottom and up the sides of pie pan. In same skillet, melt remaining 2 tablespoons butter; add onion and sauté 1-2 minutes. Spread over mushroom mixture. Sprinkle with shredded cheese. Whirl cottage cheese, eggs and cayenne pepper in blender until smooth, about 2 minutes. Pour into crust and sprinkle with paprika. Bake 20-25 minutes. Let stand 10 minutes before cutting. Serves 8.

Per serving: 250 calories; 18.5 fat grams

Mix 3-4 tablespoons crumbled bacon into crust mixture for a delicious change in flavor.

Try laying slices of fresh tomatoes on top of a quiche during the last 5 minutes of baking time.

SHRIMP QUICHE

Make this quiche as a pie for lunch entrée, or in a rectangle baking dish and cut into cubes for an hors d'oeuvres treat.

2 unbaked 9-inch pie crusts
1 cup Swiss cheese, grated
1 tablespoon flour
2 4-ounce cans small shrimp, drained
3 extra large eggs, slightly beaten
1 13-ounce can evaporated milk
1/3 cup water
2 tablespoons green onion, minced
1 tablespoon parsley flakes
1/8 teaspoon nutmeg
1/4 teaspoon salt
1/8 teaspoon pepper

Preheat oven to 350°. Prick pie crusts with fork in several places. Bake 10 minutes. In large bowl, combine 1/2 cup cheese and flour. Mix well. Sprinkle remaining cheese over bottom of each pie crust. Arrange equal amounts of shrimp over top of cheese. In large bowl, beat eggs, evaporated milk, water, onion, parsley, nutmeg, salt and pepper. Mix well. Carefully pour half of mixture over shrimp in each pie shell. Bake 40 minutes or until knife inserted in center comes out clean. Let stand 5 minutes before cutting into wedges. Serves 8.

Per serving: 353 calories; 18.3 fat grams

Quiche pans are much like spring-form pans. Be sure to spray the sides well for easy removal of the quiche.

CRAB QUICHE

Georgie loves crab in any form, and this quiche is no exception. Cyndi likes to substitute salmon for the crabmeat.

1/2 cup mayonnaise
2 tablespoons flour
2 eggs, beaten
1/2 cup half & half
1 6-ounce package crabmeat
2 cups Swiss cheese, shredded
1/3 cup green onion, chopped
1/4 cup green pepper, diced
1 4-ounce can mushroom slices or 1/2 cup
    fresh mushrooms, sliced
4 strips cooked bacon, crumbled
Pastry for 1-crust pie

Preheat oven to 350°. In large bowl, mix together mayonnaise, flour, eggs and half & half. Stir in remaining ingredients. Pour into pie crust. Bake 40-45 minutes. Let stand 5-10 minutes before cutting into wedges. Serves 6-8.

Per serving: 390 calories; 29.4 fat grams

 Fresh mushrooms don't like to be stored in plastic. Keep them refrigerated in a wire basket and use within 2-3 days.

ASPARAGUS QUICHE

Georgie's Aunt Sallie shared this great quiche recipe with us.

1 pound fresh asparagus, trimmed
Pastry for 1-crust 9-inch pie
3 tablespoons butter or margarine
3 tablespoons flour
1/2 teaspoon salt
1 1/2 cups milk
4 eggs, beaten
1/2 cup Swiss cheese
1/4 cup dry bread crumbs

Preheat oven to 450°. Cut 8 asparagus spears into 4-inch pieces; cut remaining spears into 1/2-inch pieces. Cook all in small amount of water until tender. Drain and set aside. Line pie crust with a double thickness of heavy duty foil. Bake 5 minutes. Remove foil; bake 5 minutes longer. Remove from oven and set aside. In medium saucepan over medium heat, melt butter; stir in flour and salt. Gradually add milk. Cook, stirring constantly, until thickened. Stir small amount of mixture into eggs. Slowly pour egg mixture back into pan; mix well. Stir in cheese and 1/2-inch asparagus pieces. Pour into crust. Sprinkle with bread crumbs. Bake 35 minutes or until knife inserted near center comes out clean. Arrange the 4-inch asparagus pieces in a spoke pattern on top. Serves 6-8.

Per serving: 240 calories; 15.4 fat grams

 Cook asparagus with a small amount of water in a covered, vented dish in the microwave on high 3-4 minutes.

Quiches

SPINACH PIE

Feel no guilt in eating this pie. It will make its own crust.

1 10-ounce package frozen spinach, thawed
    and well drained
1 cup Swiss cheese, shredded
1/2 cup onion, chopped
1 1/2 cups fat-free milk
3/4 cup egg substitute
3/4 cup baking mix
1 teaspoon salt
1 teaspoon pepper

Preheat oven to 400°. Spray pie plate. Mix spinach, cheese and onion in pie plate. In large mixing bowl, beat remaining ingredients until smooth. Pour mixture over spinach. Bake 30-35 minutes until knife inserted in center comes out clean. Let set 5 minutes before cutting into wedges. Serve with fresh fruit and a favorite muffin. Serves 6.

Per serving: 215 calories; 10.8 fat grams

Foot Notes

Suggested substitutions:
Add shrimp or crab to spinach mixture.
Substitute broccoli for spinach.

Rather than getting messy hands squeezing spinach dry, place spinach in a cereal bowl. Nest another cereal bowl over spinach; squeeze, tilting so water will drain off.

PECAN CRUSTED CHICKEN QUICHE

Cyndi developed this recipe to taste pretty close to the one served to her at a small restaurant in Houston. The nutty crust carries a bit of a bite.

Crust:
1/2 cup butter or margarine
1/4 cup cornmeal
3/4 cup flour
4 tablespoons paprika
1/2 teaspoon red pepper
1/2 cup pecans, finely chopped

Filling:
6 eggs
1/2 cup milk
1/2 cup Swiss cheese, shredded
2 tablespoons Parmesan cheese
4 green onions, sliced
1 cup cooked chicken, chopped
2 tablespoons dill weed
1/2 teaspoon salt

Crust:
In large bowl, melt butter in microwave on high 10-15 seconds. Add cornmeal, flour, paprika and red pepper to form pie crust consistency. Press into pie plate. Spread with pecans and press into crust.

Filling:
Preheat oven to 375°. In large bowl, beat eggs until frothy and well mixed. Add remaining ingredients. Stir well. Pour into crust. Bake 30-40 minutes until set. Let set 5 minutes before cutting into wedges. Serves 6-8.

Per serving: 337 calories; 21.4 fat grams

 Marinating or cooking chicken in buttermilk makes it more tender.

LAYERED BREAKFAST

Sunday morning brunches are popular at the Duncan home, especially after a bike ride or back nine trek. This is one of our regulars.

1 16-ounce package frozen hash browns, thawed
1 4-ounce can green chiles
1/2 cup onion, chopped
1 1/2 cups pepper cheese, shredded
1 15-ounce can refried beans
8 eggs
1/2 cup lowfat milk
Salt and pepper to taste
1/2 teaspoon oregano
1/4 teaspoon cumin
1/2 cup salsa
1 cup cheddar cheese, shredded

Fresh Pico Salsa

1 small onion
2 cloves garlic
1 jalapeño
2 green chiles or 4-ounce can chopped green chiles
3-4 sprigs cilantro
4 tomatoes, diced
1 teaspoon lime juice

Preheat oven to 350°. Spray 10 x 13-inch baking dish. In a large bowl, toss together hash browns, green chiles and onion. Spread in baking dish. Sprinkle pepper cheese over potatoes. Stir beans and spread over cheese. In the same large bowl, beat eggs, milk, salt and pepper, oregano, cumin and salsa together. Pour over beans. Bake 30 minutes. Remove from oven and top with cheddar cheese. Let stand 5 minutes before cutting. Serve with buttered tortillas, salsa and fruit. Serves 6-8.

Per serving: 396 calories; 24.2 fat grams

Fresh Pico Salsa

In food processor, whirl onion, garlic, jalapeño, green chiles and cilantro until coarsely chopped. Remove to mixing bowl. Stir in tomatoes and lime juice. Salt, if necessary.

BREAKFAST PIZZA

Our friend Becky serves this easy breakfast dish every holiday, and, on occasion, as an hors d'oeuvres.

1 pound sausage
1 package of 8 crescent rolls
1 cup hash browns, thawed
1 cup cheddar cheese, shredded, or Swiss or
    Monterey Jack
5 eggs
1/4 cup lowfat milk
1/2 teaspoon salt
1/8 teaspoon pepper
2 tablespoons Parmesan cheese

Preheat oven to 375°. Lightly spray 12-inch pizza pan. In large skillet, brown sausage; drain. Place dough on pan with points toward center. Press over bottom and up sides to form crust and seal perforations. Spoon sausage over crust. Sprinkle with potatoes then cheese. In large bowl, mix eggs, milk, salt and pepper together. Pour into crust. Top with Parmesan cheese. Bake 25-30 minutes. Serves 6.

Per serving: 562 calories; 40.8 fat grams

Foot Notes

Use a salad spinner to dry hash browns QUICKly.

Do any of you remember when Oprah was so excited about fat free potato chips? Well, guess what? There are now fat free hash browns! We will definitely try those in some of our recipes.

HEIDI'S BREAKFAST CASSEROLE

Heidi, who says that she is not a cook, always comes up with great recipes that the Duncan family asks for over and over. This recipe is easy to fix the night before.

12 ounces sausage links
10 corn tortillas
3/4 cup Monterey Jack cheese, shredded
3/4 cup sharp cheddar cheese, shredded
1 4-ounce can diced green chiles
1 tomato, diced
3 eggs
3/4 cup milk
1 teaspoon chili powder
1/2 teaspoon salt
Avocado or cilantro, optional

Preheat oven to 350°. Spray 9-inch pie plate. In small skillet, cook sausage; drain. Cut into 1/2-inch pieces. Place 9 tortillas in pie plate overlapping edges and extending about 1/2-inch above rim. Place 1 tortilla in center. Combine sausage and cheeses. Spread over tortillas. Add chiles and tomatoes. Beat eggs, milk, salt and chili powder together. Pour over ingredients in pie plate. Bake 35-40 minutes. Serves 6.

Per serving: 499 calories; 36.1 fat grams

Foot Note When shredding cheese, spray the grater first to prevent cheese from sticking to it. The difference between 'grating' and 'shredding' is that the larger holes on a grater are used for shredding. Grating produces finer particles.

CRAB BAKE

This is an easy, make-ahead recipe when time is of the essence.

1/2 cup mayonnaise
2 7-ounce cans crab meat
1 onion, chopped
1 green pepper, chopped
1 cup celery, chopped
3 cups milk
4 eggs, beaten
8 slices white bread
1 cup mushroom soup, undiluted
1 cup sharp cheddar cheese

Spray 9 x 13-inch baking dish. In large bowl, combine first 7 ingredients. Dice 4 slices of bread with crusts and spread in baking dish. Pour crab mixture over top. Lay 4 slices of bread without crusts on top. Cover and refrigerate overnight. Preheat oven to 325°. Bake 15 minutes. Remove and spoon soup over top. Sprinkle with cheese. Bake 1 hour more. Serves 8.

Per serving: 399 calories; 24.7 fat grams

 Hamburger, pepperoni, ham or chicken could be substituted for the crab meat. Or, you can make it meatless and add chunks of zucchini instead of the crab.

MEXICAN STRATA

This tasty dish is good any time of the day.

2 cups cheese flavored tortilla chips, broken
1 1/2 cups sharp cheddar, Monterey Jack or
    pepper jack cheese, shredded
1/2 pound sausage or chorizo, browned and
    well drained
8 eggs, beaten
1/2 cup milk
1 7-ounce can chopped green chiles
1/2 cup onion, chopped
1 clove garlic, minced
1/2 teaspoon salt
1/2 teaspoon hot pepper sauce
3 tablespoons catsup

Spray 9 x 13-inch baking dish. Spread tortilla chips over bottom of dish. Sprinkle cheese over chips. Spoon sausage evenly over cheese. In large bowl, beat eggs. Stir in remaining ingredients. Pour over sausage. Cover with foil and refrigerate overnight. Preheat oven to 325°. Remove foil from casserole. Bake 50-55 minutes. Offer condiments of salsa, sour cream, black olives, onions and tomatoes. Serves 8.

Per serving: 477 calories; 27.9 fat grams

Foot Note Omit the sausage and substitute ham or Canadian bacon, if desired. Douse with a good helping of green chile for extra flavor.

OVERNIGHT ARTICHOKE BAKE

The English muffin crust makes this dish extraordinary.

3 English muffins, split and quartered
1 tablespoon butter or margarine, melted
1 cup lean ham, chopped
1/2 cup fresh Parmesan cheese, grated
1 green onion, chopped
1 14-ounce can artichoke hearts, drained
    and chopped
3 large cloves garlic, minced
1/8 teaspoon nutmeg
1 12-ounce can evaporated fat-free milk
3 large eggs
3 large egg whites

Spray 8 x 8-inch baking dish. Arrange muffin pieces crust sides down in dish. Drizzle with butter. In large bowl, mix ham, Parmesan cheese, onion, artichoke hearts and garlic together. Spoon over muffin pieces. In large bowl, whisk remaining ingredients thoroughly. Pour over muffin mixture. Cover. Chill at least 8 hours or overnight. Preheat oven to 375°. Uncover and bake 50 minutes. Let stand 10 minutes. Serves 6.

Per serving: 272 calories; 8.0 fat grams

Flavor enhancing nutmeg is the secret ingredient in many recipes, including chilis and soups.

HASH BROWN AND EGG SKILLET

This is a one-dish recipe using egg substitute.

2 cups hash brown potatoes
1/4 cup fresh cilantro, chopped
1/2 cup onion, chopped
1/2 cup cheddar cheese, shredded
1/2 cup Mexican processed cheese, grated
1 10-ounce can green chiles and tomatoes
8 eggs, beaten
1/4 cup milk
Salt and pepper to taste
1/2 teaspoon oregano
Salsa, if desired

Preheat oven to 375°. Spray medium oven-proof skillet. Layer first six ingredients in skillet. In medium mixing bowl, beat together next four ingredients. Pour over potatoes. Bake 30 minutes. Let stand 5 minutes before cutting into four pieces. Offer salsa as garnish. Serves 4.

Per serving: 414 calories; 27.3 fat grams

 Keep cilantro fresh by trimming stems and placing in glass of water. Cover with plastic bag or wrap. Store in refrigerator 3-4 weeks and use as needed.

SCRAMBLED EGG CASSEROLE

Make this casserole for a crowd. Think ahead; this needs to set overnight.

2 1/2 tablespoons flour
2 tablespoons butter or margarine, melted
2 cups milk
1/2 teaspoon salt
1/4 teaspoon pepper
1 8-ounce package light cream cheese, cubed
1/4 cup green onions, chopped
3 tablespoons butter or margarine, melted
12 eggs, beaten
1/2 teaspoon salt
1/2 teaspoon pepper
1 4-ounce can sliced mushrooms, drained
2 1/4 cups bread crumbs
1/2 cup butter or margarine
1/4 teaspoon paprika

Spray 9 x 13-inch baking dish. In heavy saucepan, blend flour and 2 tablespoons butter; cook 1 minute. Add milk gradually. Cook over medium heat until thickened, stirring constantly. Add 1/2 teaspoon salt, 1/4 teaspoon pepper and cream cheese. Mix until smooth. Remove from heat. In large skillet, sauté green onions in 3 tablespoons butter. Add eggs, 1/2 teaspoon salt and 1/2 teaspoon pepper. Cook until barely set, stirring often. Add mushrooms and cheese sauce. Spoon into baking dish. Toss bread crumbs with 1/2 cup melted butter. Spread over casserole and sprinkle with paprika. Cover and chill overnight. Preheat oven to 350°. Bake 30 minutes or until heated through. Serves 12.

Per serving: 303 calories; 19.2 fat grams

 Use fresh bread crumbs for crispier coating on pan fried foods since they absorb less oil. Dry bread crumbs are better for stuffings and fillings because they absorb liquids.

DEVILED EGGS IN CHEESE SAUCE

Put leftover Easter eggs to good use (after the hunt) in this tasty little dish.

6 hard-cooked eggs, sliced lengthwise
1/2 teaspoon dry mustard
1/2 teaspoon salt
1/4 teaspoon pepper
3 tablespoons salad dressing
Mushrooms, chopped, optional
Shrimp, chopped, optional
2 tablespoons butter or margarine
2 tablespoons flour
1 cup milk
Cheese to taste

Preheat oven to 350°. Spray 8 x 8-inch baking dish. Remove egg yolks to small bowl; mash with fork. Blend in mustard, salt, pepper and salad dressing. Spoon mixture into egg whites; arrange eggs in casserole dish. Top with mushrooms and shrimp. Mix butter, flour and milk in double boiler; cook, stirring, until smooth and creamy. Stir in cheese until melted. Pour over eggs. Bake 20 minutes. Serves 6.

Per serving: 194 calories; 14.8 fat grams

 To make perfect hard-cooked eggs, place cold eggs in single layer in saucepan and cover with 1-inch water. Cover pan and bring to boil over medium-high heat. Immediately remove the pan from the heat. Let the eggs stand in hot water 12-15 minutes. Pour hot water off and cover with cold or ice water to stop the cooking process. Let cool completely before peeling eggs under cold running water.

SALLIE'S EGG CASSEROLE

"My kids love this if we have Easter brunch," says our pal Sal. "I like it best with sausage or bacon."

1 cup ham, bacon or sausage
1/4 cup onion, chopped
12 eggs
1 4-ounce can mushrooms
Cheese Sauce (recipe below)
1 1/2 tablespoons butter or margarine
2 1/4 cups soft bread crumbs
Paprika

Cheese Sauce:
2 tablespoons butter or margarine
2 tablespoons flour
2 cups milk
1 cup American processed cheese

Spray 9 x 13-inch baking dish. In large sprayed skillet, cook meat and onion; drain. Add eggs and scramble just until almost set. Fold in mushrooms and cheese sauce. Spoon into baking dish. In small bowl, melt 1 1/2 tablespoons butter in microwave. Toss with bread crumbs. Spread over egg mixture. Sprinkle with paprika. Refrigerate 30 minutes. Bake, uncovered, 30 minutes. Serves 8.

Cheese Sauce:
In small sauce pan, melt butter; add flour. Stir and cook 1 minute. Gradually add milk, stirring constantly. Add cheese and stir until melted.

Per serving: 290 calories; 20.0 fat grams

BACON AND SWISS BRUNCH PIE

Unusual ingredients in this pie hit numerous facets of a nutritious breakfast all in one.

8 slices bacon
1 tablespoon bacon drippings
1/2 cup corn flake crumbs
5 eggs
2 1/2 cups frozen hash brown potatoes, thawed and uncooked
1 1/2 cups Swiss cheese, shredded
1/2 cup cottage cheese
1/3 cup milk
1 green onion with tops, thinly sliced
1/4 teaspoon salt
Pepper to taste
4 drops red pepper sauce

Spray 9-inch pie pan. Microwave bacon until crisp. Crumble. In small bowl, thoroughly mix bacon drippings with corn flakes. Set aside. In medium bowl, beat eggs until foamy. Stir in potatoes, cheeses, milk, onion, salt, pepper and red pepper sauce. Pour into pie pan. Sprinkle with cereal mixture and bacon. Cover and refrigerate overnight. Preheat oven to 325°. Uncover pie and bake 1 hour. Let stand 5 minutes before cutting. Serves 6.

Per serving: 393 calories; 26.0 fat grams

 Microwave bacon on sprayed microwave bacon dish or paper plate covered with paper towels. Layer 4-5 slices with 2 sheets of paper toweling between layers. Microwave on high 4 minutes. Check and set again at shorter intervals until bacon is crisp. Remove any pieces that are crisp before others.

MEATLESS BREAKFAST BURRITOS

Depending on how many varieties you make, you could have a different flavor every day. Make extras and freeze so you can serve them any time.

6-8 potatoes, boiled, cubed or shredded
Salt and pepper to taste
1 cup refried beans
1 teaspoon chili powder
1 teaspoon cayenne pepper
1 cup salsa
1 cup cheddar, Monterey Jack or combination of cheeses, grated
1 onion, chopped
1 7-ounce can diced green chiles
1 tablespoon butter
8 eggs, beaten
Salt and pepper to taste
12 flour tortillas, warmed between two damp paper towels 30 seconds on high in microwave

In large bowl, mix potatoes, salt, pepper, beans, chili powder, cayenne pepper, salsa and cheese. Set aside. In large skillet, sauté onion and green chiles in butter. Add eggs, salt and pepper. Scramble until slightly creamy. Combine with potato mixture. Fill tortillas, about 3/4 way down centers, with 2-3 heaping tablespoonfuls of mixture. Fold up bottom edge of tortilla, then fold left and right edges over mixture, leaving top open to add extra salsa. Serve hot (microwave for short time to reheat). To make crispy burritos bake them in the oven about 10 minutes. Serves 12.

Per serving: 275 calories; 10.6 fat grams

 To freeze, wrap each snugly in plastic wrap and place in freezer bag. Defrost in refrigerator or by microwaving at 1 minute intervals (microwaving too long will make tortilla tough).

Plan ahead and boil potatoes while preparing another meal. Use potato masher to make chunky mixture. Refrigerate until ready to use.

HUEVOS RANCHEROS

This is absolutely one of the Duncan household favorites as is any Mexican food dish.

4 large flour tortillas
1 15-ounce can refried beans (or 2 cups of
    your own homemade beans), or black
    beans
2 cups green chili (recipe follows)
2 cups cheddar cheese, grated
4-8 eggs (depending on how many each
    person wants)
2 tablespoons butter or margarine
Salsa

Green Chili
1 large onion, chopped
4 cloves garlic, minced
1/2 teaspoon cayenne pepper
2 tablespoons olive oil
1 16-ounce can whole green chiles, cut in
    large strips
3-4 tablespoons jalapeño peppers (depend-
    ing on how much heat you like)
3 cups water
1 tomato, diced

Lay each tortilla on dinner plate. Spread each with equal portions of refried beans. Spoon equal amounts of green chili over the top and spread 1/2 cup cheese on each. Cover with plastic wrap and microwave on high 1 minute or until cheese melts. While microwaving, fry eggs in butter to order. Place eggs on top. Spoon a tablespoon or two of salsa on top of egg. Serve hot with orange slices and/or pan-fried hash brown potatoes and salsa on the side. Serves 4.

Per serving: 614 calories; 35.5 fat grams

Green Chili
In large skillet, sauté onion, garlic and cayenne in olive oil. Add green chiles, jalapeños and water. Simmer 10 minutes. Add tomato. Can be used on any Mexican food entrée, eggs or steaks. If you prefer a thicker green chili, combine 2 tablespoons cornstarch and 3 tablespoons water. Stir into hot mixture and stir until thickened. Makes 5-6 cups.

VEGETABLE HASH

You know how sometimes breakfast tastes so good for dinner? This hash goes perfectly with thick slices of toasted homemade bread, or big, hot biscuits.

4 medium potatoes, peeled and cut into 1/2-inch cubes
2 cups water
6 slices bacon, cut into 1-inch pieces
1 large red pepper, cut into 1/2-inch pieces
1/4 teaspoon salt
1 15-ounce can black beans, rinsed and drained
4 large eggs
Enough water to cover eggs while cooking

In medium pan, bring potatoes and water to a boil. Reduce heat, cover and simmer 4 minutes, until potatoes are tender. Drain well. In large skillet, cook bacon; drain. Add pepper, potatoes, salt and beans. Heat through, turning occasionally to prevent burning. In large skillet, heat 1 1/2-inches water to boiling. Reduce heat to simmer. To poach eggs, break each into custard cup. Holding cup close to water, slip egg into simmering water. Spoon hash onto the serving plate. Wait until the egg starts to rise in the water before scooping out with a slotted spoon, about 3-5 minutes. Drain bottom of spoon on paper towel. Slip egg from spoon onto hash. Serves 6.

Per serving: 368 calories; 7.0 fat grams

 Add a little vinegar to the simmering water. The acid makes the white cook faster.

EGGS BENEDICT

This original French recipe came into New Orleans many years ago as a delicacy and is still a well-known favorite everywhere. Bring it into your home and make it your favorite.

1 English muffin
1 slice Canadian bacon or ham
1 egg, poached
3-4 tablespoons Hollandaise Sauce

Hollandaise Sauce
2 egg yolks
1 tablespoon fresh lemon juice
1/2 cup butter, divided into 3 pieces

Mock Hollandaise Sauce
1/4 cup sour cream
1/4 cup plain yogurt
1 teaspoon lemon juice
1/2 teaspoon prepared mustard

Toast English muffin. Butter if desired. Place Canadian bacon on bottom slice of muffin. Poach egg in boiling water or in poacher. Scoop with slotted spoon, drain and place on top of bacon. Spoon generous portion of Hollandaise sauce. Repeat for number of guests present. Serves 1.

Hollandaise Sauce: Combine egg yolks and lemon juice in top of double boiler over hot, not boiling water. Add butter, 1 piece at a time, stirring constantly until melted. Continue stirring until thickened. Makes 3/4 cup.

Mock Hollandaise Sauce: In small pan, combine all ingredients. Cook and stir over very low heat till heated through (DO NOT boil) and thickened. Makes 1/2 cup.

Per serving:
Hollandaise Sauce: *484 calories; 33.3 fat grams*
Mock Hollandaise Sauce: *293 calories; 11.5 fat grams*

BUTTERMILK BISCUITS AND SAUSAGE GRAVY

This is probably close to the All-American favorite, right at the top with Chicken Fried Steak. To stream-line prep work, Georgie uses frozen Southern Style Biscuits and bakes only what is needed.

Biscuits
2 cups flour
3 teaspoons baking powder
1 teaspoon salt
1/3 cup shortening
3/4 cup buttermilk

Sausage Gravy
1/4 pound sausage
1-2 tablespoons oil
3-4 tablespoons flour
1 teaspoon salt
1/2 teaspoon ground pepper
3-4 cups lowfat milk (quantity depends on
    how thick you like gravy)

Biscuits
Preheat oven to 425°. In large bowl, mix flour, baking powder and salt together. Cut in shortening with fork or pastry blender. Stir in buttermilk, just until moistened. On floured surface, knead 10 times. (This helps activate the baking powder). Pat out to 1-1 1/2-inch thick. Cut with biscuit cutter, cookie cutter or open end of glass. Place on ungreased cookie sheet. Bake 8-10 minutes. Split and serve hot with gravy. Serves 6.

Sausage Gravy
In large skillet, brown sausage. Add enough oil to mix with flour, salt and pepper. Brown slightly over high heat. Gradually add milk, stirring constantly until thickened. Dilute with extra milk or water, if needed.

Per serving: 365 calories; 16.8 fat grams

FRUIT SAUCE

Use favorite fruit to make delicious toppings for pancakes, waffles, biscuits, French toast, or ice cream.

2 tablespoons sugar
1 tablespoon cornstarch
1 1/2 tablespoons water
1/2 teaspoon lemon juice
1/4 teaspoon cinnamon
1 1/2-2 cups fruit (blueberries, raspberries,
    blackberries, peaches), or 1 10-ounce
    package frozen fruit, thawed
1/4 teaspoon almond extract or vanilla

In medium pan, stir sugar, cornstarch, water, lemon juice and cinnamon until smooth. Add fruit. Bring to boil and cook 2 minutes until thickened. Remove from heat. Stir in extract. Cover and keep warm on lowest heat until ready to serve. Serves 6.

Per serving: 32 calories; 0.1 fat grams

 Apples need a little more cooking than the above fruits. Place 1 1/2-2 cups apples in pan with 4 tablespoons sugar (or brown sugar), 1/2 cup water, 1/2 teaspoon lemon juice, 1/2 teaspoon cinnamon and 1/2 teaspoon apple pie spice. Cook 10-15 minutes to desired tenderness. Mix cornstarch with 1 1/2 tablespoons water. Stir into apples and cook until thickened. Do not add extract.

PEEK-A-BOO TOAST

Make your children/grandchildren giggle with this fun dish. Surround with their favorite fruit. Cyndi's husband likes toast covered with jam and a poached egg on top-about the same-only with flair.

1 slice firm white, whole wheat, or brown
    bread
1 tablespoon butter or margarine
1 egg
Salt and freshly ground pepper, optional
Paprika, optional

Cut a 2-inch hole in the center of the bread with a biscuit cutter, cookie cutter or open end of a glass. In small skillet, melt butter over medium heat. Place bread slice in skillet and 'toast' until golden on bottom side. Turn bread over, crack egg into custard dish and pour gently into hole. Sprinkle with salt and pepper. Cover pan and cook 1 minute. Uncover and cook 1 minute more, or until cooked to preference. Dust with paprika. Serves 1.

Per serving: 230 calories; 16.5 fat grams

 Make Peek-a-Boo French Toast by whisking 1 egg and 2 tablespoons water together. Season with dash of salt, cinnamon and vanilla. Dip bread with hole into egg mixture and continue as directed above.

Miscellaneous Brunch Dishes

GRANOLA PANCAKES

For years Cyndi and Georgie made their own mixes for pancakes. Now there are a variety of prepackaged mixes that can be used as the basis for creating tasty pancakes.

1 1/2 cups pancake mix (original, butter-
    milk, whole wheat; it doesn't matter)
3/4-1 cup water
1/2 cup oatmeal
1/2 cup crunchy cereal nuggets
1/2 cup almonds
1/2 cup dried fruit (cherries, cranberries,
    apples, bananas or a mixture)
2 tablespoons butter, melted, or oil
Butter for cooking on griddle

Preheat and spray griddle. In large bowl, mix all ingredients, except the butter for cooking. Do not overmix. Pour batter by 1/4 cupfuls onto hot buttered griddle. Turn when bubbles form on top of pancakes. Cook until second side is golden brown. Serve with yogurt, fruit compote, syrup or jam. Serves 6.

Per serving: 265 calories; 7.3 fat grams

To make dessert **Pancake Rollups**, thin batter slightly by adding more water. Spoon favorite fruit pie filling in center of cooked pancake. Roll up, place on serving plate and top with whipped topping spiced up with a little cinnamon and maple syrup.

OATMEAL WHEAT WAFFLES

Want to dress up your waffles? Serve with flavored butters, fresh fruits and cream, or cooked fruit compotes.

2 eggs, beaten
1 1/2 cups buttermilk
1/2 cup club soda (make waffles and pancakes lighter)
1 cup quick-cooking oats
1 tablespoon molasses
1 tablespoon oil
1 cup whole wheat flour
1/2 teaspoon salt
1 teaspoon baking soda
1 teaspoon baking powder

Preheat waffle maker. In large bowl, mix eggs, buttermilk and club soda. Add remaining ingredients, stir well but do not overmix. Thin batter by adding a little milk. Thicken by adding a little more flour. Spray waffle iron. Bake until light goes off or nicely browned. Top with warm syrup. Serves 6.

Per serving: 195 calories; 5.5 fat grams

 Suggestions for flavored butters:

Strawberry Butter: to 1/2 cup butter add 1/4 cup strawberry jam and 1/2 teaspoon lemon juice.
Honey Butter: To 1/2 cup butter add 1/4 cup honey and 1/2 teaspoon cinnamon.
Orange Butter: To 1/2 cup butter add 1/3 cup orange marmalade, 1/2 teaspoon finely grated fresh orange peel and 3 tablespoons nuts.
Bacon Butter: To 1/2 cup butter add 3/4 teaspoon mustard and 1/4 cup crumbled bacon. (This one is great on baked potatoes, too).

LOWFAT FRENCH TOAST

Lowfat? Using French or Italian breads which are lower in fat than other breads, reducing the number of egg yolks to cut cholesterol and topping with fresh fruit makes this recipe a healthy choice.

1 large egg
2 egg whites
1/4 cup skim milk
1/2 teaspoon vanilla
1/2 teaspoon cinnamon
1/8 teaspoon nutmeg
8 1-inch-thick slices French or Italian
    bread, diagonally cut
Cinnamon sugar, reduced calorie maple
    syrup and powdered sugar, optional

Preheat large griddle. In pie plate, whisk egg and egg whites until frothy. Add milk, vanilla, cinnamon and nutmeg. Beat well and set aside. Preheat oven to 200°. Spray griddle or large nonstick skillet. Whisk egg mixture before each dipping to mix spices. Dip bread slices into egg mixture, turning to coat and draining excess back into dish. Place on griddle or in skillet. Cook until golden brown, turning once. Transfer to plate and keep in warm oven until remaining slices are cooked. Serve immediately with cinnamon sugar, powdered sugar, syrup, or fruit and cream. Serves 4.

Per serving: 168 calories; 2.6 fat grams

For **Custard French Toast**, prepare egg mixture in a large 10 x 15-inch glass baking dish. Add bread slices, turning to coat. Cover and refrigerate overnight. Cook as above.

Substitute raisin, whole wheat, pumpkin or banana bread for variety.

STUFFED FRENCH TOAST

This resembles a banana split without the ice cream, served hot.

1 10-ounce jar maraschino cherries, without stems
1 8-ounce package cream cheese, softened
1/4 cup sugar
1 teaspoon vanilla
1 8-ounce can crushed pineapple in juice, drained well
1/3 cup miniature chocolate chips
1 16-ounce loaf French bread, sliced into 16 1/2-3/4-inch pieces
4 eggs
1/3 cup milk
4 small ripe bananas, sliced lengthwise
2 cups whipped topping
1/4 cup pecans, chopped, optional
Maple syrup, warmed

Preheat oven to 350°. Spray large baking sheet with sides. Cut 4 cherries in half; set aside for garnish. Chop remaining cherries. In medium bowl, combine cream cheese, sugar and vanilla; beat until creamy. Stir in pineapple, chocolate chips and chopped cherries. In pie plate, beat eggs with milk. Dip one side of 8 slices of bread in egg mixture. Place on baking sheet, dipped side down. Gently spread each slice with cream cheese mixture. Top with banana half. Dip one side of each remaining bread slices in egg mixture. Place dipped side up, on top of bananas. Bake 35-40 minutes, or until tops are light golden brown and center is set. Top each serving with whipped cream, pecans and 1 cherry half. Serve with maple syrup. Serves 8.

Per serving: 503 calories; 21.2 fat grams

 Mix blueberries with cream cheese, sugar and lemon juice. Omit cherries, pineapple, chocolate chips and bananas. 'Stuff' as instructed.

TEXAS FRENCH TOAST

The flavor of this dish is similar to the popular créme brulée, Georgie's favorite. It's a tasty combination of caramelized sugar and custard base.

2/3 cup maple syrup
1/3 cup brown sugar
1/4 cup butter or margarine
1 1/2 teaspoons vanilla
Dash of salt
12 slices Texas Toast without crusts, or
    soft-textured egg bread
8 eggs
1 cup milk or cream

Preheat oven to 350°. Spray 9 x 12-inch baking dish. In medium pan, combine syrup, brown sugar and butter. Cook over medium heat until caramelized. Add vanilla and salt. Pour caramel sauce in baking dish. Place slices of toast on top of sauce. In large bowl, beat eggs and milk. Pour over toast. Refrigerate overnight. Bake 45 minutes, until mixture sets. Remove from oven, let set 2-3 minutes and slice. To serve, flip each slice over so sauce is on top. Serves 6.

Per serving: 433 calories; 16.5 fat grams

 Caramelizing sugar means to cook over medium heat until bubbly and browned, stirring constantly.

BLUEBERRY FRENCH TOAST

Served with the blueberry sauce or 'plain ole' maple syrup, this French toast is delicious.

12 slices day old bread without crusts, or
    French bread, cubed
1 8-ounce package light cream cheese
8 eggs
1 1/2 cups lowfat milk
1/4 cup maple syrup

Blueberry Sauce

1 cup sugar
1 tablespoon butter or margarine
2 tablespoons cornstarch
1 cup water
2 cups blueberries
1 teaspoon vanilla
1 tablespoon maple syrup

Spray 9 x 13-inch baking dish. Place 1/2 bread in baking dish. Cut cream cheese into pieces and drop over bread. Cover with remaining bread. In large bowl, beat eggs until creamy. Stir in milk and maple syrup; pour over bread mixture. Cover and chill overnight. Take out of refrigerator 30 minutes before baking. Bake 30 minutes, covered. Uncover and bake another 30 minutes. Serve each piece with blueberry sauce or maple syrup on top. Serves 8.

Blueberry Sauce
Prepare while 'toast' is baking. In medium pan, combine first five ingredients. Cook until of syrup consistency. Stir in vanilla and maple syrup.

Per serving: 418 calories, 12.7 fat grams

This blueberry sauce is good served over pancakes, waffles, biscuits or ice cream. Try substituting raspberries or blackberries for the blueberries. Yum.

Notes:

Lunches

BAKED HAM & SWISS SANDWICHES

Prepare, heat and eat, or prepare, wrap and freeze. Keep a supply on hand in the freezer for emergency lunches.

1/2 cup butter or margarine
1 1/2 teaspoons poppy seeds
1 tablespoon Worcestershire sauce
1 tablespoon onion flakes
1 tablespoon prepared mustard
4 Kaiser rolls
4 ham slices for sandwiches
4 slices Swiss cheese

Preheat oven to 350°. Spray cookie sheet. In medium bowl, mix butter, poppy seeds, Worcestershire sauce, onion flakes and mustard. Mix well. Slice rolls. Spread butter mixture on both pieces of each roll. Place ham and cheese slices on each roll. Cover with other piece of roll. Wrap loosely in foil. Place on cookie sheet and bake 15 minutes. Serve with favorite soup. Serves 4.

Per serving: 466 calories; 34.2 fat grams

 To freeze, first wrap in plastic wrap, then in foil. Place in zippered bag. Freeze up to 3 months.

ASPARAGUS HAM SANDWICHES

The leftover Easter ham in the refrigerator and a beautiful spring crop of asparagus were the inspirations behind this recipe. They are great made with rye bread, too.

2 tablespoons butter or margarine, softened
3/4 teaspoon garlic powder
1/2 teaspoon parsley
6 1-inch thick slices French, sour dough or
   rye bread
1 cup extra lean ham, chopped
1 cup Swiss cheese, shredded
1 cup light mayonnaise or salad dressing
2 tablespoons Dijon mustard
2 tablespoons dry white wine
1/2 pound fresh asparagus spears, cooked

Preheat oven to broil. Spray baking sheet lightly. In small bowl, combine butter, garlic powder and parsley. Spread on each side of bread slice. Place on baking sheet. Broil 4 inches from heat 2 minutes or until lightly toasted. In medium bowl, mix ham, cheese, mayonnaise, mustard and wine. Layer bread slices with cooked asparagus spears and ham mixture. Broil 4-5 minutes, until thoroughly heated and lightly browned. Serves 6.

Per serving: 255 calories; 13.2 fat grams

Foot Note Choose asparagus with tightly closed tips and deep green and/or purplish color. The stalks should be firm with taut skin (none of that wrinkly stuff). It should stand up straight when held from the bottom. To store wrap stalk bottoms in damp paper towel, then wrap in foil. Asparagus will stay crisp and flavorful for 2-4 days.

HOT HAM HOAGIES

This sandwich is very versatile. You can use ham, chicken, turkey, tuna or salmon with delicious results.

10-ounces extra lean ham, cubed
1/4 cup light mayonnaise
1/4 cup light sour cream
2 tablespoons onion, chopped
2 tablespoons parsley
1/4 teaspoon garlic salt
1/2 French bread loaf
3 tablespoons butter or margarine
1 green pepper, sliced horizontally
1 cup cheddar cheese, shredded
1/4 cup black olives, sliced

Turn oven to broil. Spray large baking sheet. In large bowl, combine ham, mayonnaise, sour cream, onion, parsley and garlic salt. Slice bread lengthwise and place on baking sheet. (To keep from 'rocking', slice off small rounded piece on bottom of bread). Butter each half. Lay 3-4 pieces of green pepper on each. Spread with meat mixture. Cover with cheese. Garnish with 3-4 more pieces of green pepper. Arrange olive slices in center of peppers. Broil until cheese is bubbly, about 5 minutes. Serves 4.

Per serving: 474 calories; 25.5 fat grams

 Freeze washed, stemmed and seeded green peppers in freezer bag. When ready to use, 'smash' into pieces with rubber meat mallet.

PATRICK DELI HOAGIES

Need a QUICK meal, ask Georgie for her best deli recipes.

6-8 hoagie buns
3/4 pound honey baked ham
3/4 pound oven roasted turkey
1/2 pound pastrami
8 slices American cheese
2 tomatoes, sliced
Lettuce leaves
Red onion, sliced, optional
1/2 cup light salad dressing or Italian dress-
    ing, or mixture of both
Brown mustard, optional

Slice hoagie buns lengthwise. Layer ingredients in order given. Offer dressings and mustard on the side. Serves 6-8.

Per serving: 466 calories; 27.5 fat grams

 Try different dressings on these sandwiches. Here is a good one if you like horseradish:

Horseradish Mayo

1 cup light mayonnaise
1/4 cup prepared horseradish
2 teaspoons Dijon mustard
1 clove garlic, minced
1 teaspoon lemon juice
1/4 teaspoon cayenne pepper
Mix all ingredients. Chill. This is a good binder for tuna, egg or salmon salads, or as a spread on wraps.

ZESTY ITALIAN SUBS

Hoagies, sub sandwiches, poor boys. . . what is the difference?

1/4 cup creamy Italian or cheesy salad
    dressing
2 tablespoons grated Parmesan cheese
1 14-ounce can artichoke hearts in water,
    drained and quartered
1 cup cherry tomatoes, halved
1 5-ounce package thinly sliced pepperoni
1 2-ounce can sliced black olives, drained
1/2 cup red or green onions, chopped
2 10-inch hoagie rolls
1/2-1 cup shredded mozzarella cheese

In medium bowl, combine dressing and cheese. Add artichokes, tomatoes, pepperoni, olives and onions. Toss to coat. Cut each roll in half lengthwise. Place cut side up on ungreased baking sheet. Set oven to broil. Broil 5 inches from heat for 1 minute. Spread filling over rolls. Sprinkle with mozzarella. Broil 3-4 minutes longer until filling is hot and cheese is bubbly. Watch carefully. Serves 4.

Per serving: 327 calories; 23.1 fat grams

 Think out of the box for unusual dressings for sandwiches and salads.

<u>Sun-dried Tomato Dressing</u>

1 cup light mayonnaise
6 sundried tomato pieces
2 cloves garlic, chopped
1 green onion, chopped
6 basil leaves
1 tablespoon chili sauce
Whirl in blender until smooth. Salt and pepper if necessary.

MEATBALL SANDWICHES

Georgie cooks extra meatballs and sauce when making spaghetti, so Bob can indulge in this favorite.

1 pound extra lean ground beef
1/2 cup dry Italian style bread crumbs
1 egg, slightly beaten
1 clove garlic, minced
1/3 cup Parmesan cheese
1 tablespoon parsley
1 teaspoon salt
1/2 teaspoon freshly ground pepper
1 tablespoon Italian seasoning
2-3 tablespoons oil
1 16-ounce jar pasta sauce, or make your
    own
8 French bread rolls, about 6 inches long
8 slices mozzarella cheese

In large bowl, combine beef, bread crumbs, egg, garlic, cheese, parsley, salt, pepper and seasoning. Mix well. Shape into 8 or 9 large balls. Thoroughly brown meatballs on all sides in oil. Drain well on paper toweling. In large pan, place meatballs in pasta sauce. Cover, heat and simmer 20-30 minutes. Split rolls lengthwise. Spoon 2-3 tablespoons pasta sauce on bread. Slice meatballs in half and arrange on bottom halves of roll. Spoon desired amount of sauce on top. Place 2 slices of cheese on top of meat. Close sandwiches with top halves of rolls. Serve hot with extra sauce, or wrap individually for picnics or camping trips. Garnish with slices of green and red peppers and onion. Serves 12.

Per serving: 348 calories; 21.5 fat grams

 To save some calories, serve this sandwich open-faced using only 4 rolls.

PIZZA BURGERS

Think ahead and cook beef early. We usually cook 2 pounds of ground beef at once, using 1 pound for the recipe at hand and freezing the other pound for another meal. This could be that other meal.

1 pound extra lean ground beef, cooked, drained and cooled
1 cup Monterey Jack cheese, shredded
1 cup mozzarella, shredded
Onion salt to taste
1/2 cup black olives, chopped
1/2 teaspoon oregano
1/4 teaspoon garlic salt
1/2 cup condensed tomato soup
6 slices Vienna bread

Spray large baking sheet. In large bowl, combine all ingredients, except bread, and mix well. Chill 1 hour. Spread on Vienna bread slices and place on baking sheet. Set oven to broil. Heat under broiler until hot and bubbly. Serves 6.

Per serving: 401 calories; 25.4 fat grams

Try making this into a Vegetarian Pizza Burger by adding lots of fresh vegetables in place of the ground beef. Or, use different meats like Italian sausage or pepperoni.

SLOPPY JOES

Cyndi's grandson, Tommy, asks for sloppy joes almost every time he comes to visit. And Cyndi does what Grandmas do, fixes it!! The recipe came from her husband's mother, a matriarch of grandmothership.

4 pounds extra lean ground beef or turkey
2 1/2 cups onions, chopped
1 15-ounce crushed tomatoes, optional, or
    tomato soup, optional (Cyndi omits this
    ingredient when fixing for Tommy)
2 1/2 cups catsup
4 tablespoons chili powder
2 tablespoons dry mustard
1 teaspoon salt
1 teaspoon pepper
16-20 hamburger buns

In large skillet, cook beef, drain well. Add remaining ingredients, except buns, and simmer 15-20 minutes. Serve on hamburger buns with cottage cheese and dill pickles (that's the way the Duncans like them). Serves 16-20.

Per serving: 415 calories; 20.0 fat grams

Foot Notes

There's enough here for 2-3 meals, depending on how many you are serving, so freeze in suitable portions for that QUICK meal at another time.

For a little change from sloppy joes, spread mixture on pizza dough and top with cheese and other favorite pizza ingredients.

BARBECUE BURGERS AND SALSA

We've made a lot of salsas, but never one with barbecue sauce, until we found this recipe. The salsa can be prepared ahead and used with other meals like stuffed potatoes.

1 1/2 pounds extra lean ground beef
1/2 cup crushed corn chips
1/4 cup barbecue sauce
3 tablespoons chopped green chiles, well-
    drained
2 tablespoons onion, chopped
Salsa

Barbecue Salsa

1 8-ounce can Mexi-corn, drained
1/2 cup tomato, chopped
2/3 cup barbecue sauce
1/2 cup celery, chopped
1/4 cup green pepper, chopped
1/4 cup onion, chopped

Start grill. In large bowl, combine meat, chips, barbecue sauce, chiles and onion. Mix lightly. Shape into 6 patties. Grill on both sides to desired doneness. Top with salsa before serving or serve on the side. Offer hamburger buns and serve with plenty of vegetables and potatoes, if desired. Serves 6.

Barbecue Salsa

Combine all ingredients. Mix well. Serves 6.

Per serving: 434 calories; 26.9 fat grams

 These burgers are good with chicken substituted for beef and can be grilled inside, under broiler, brushing frequently with barbecue sauce, to desired doneness.

CURRIED BEEF PITAS

Although Cyndi loves zucchini, she likes to use asparagus, mushrooms and potatoes with chicken or left-over pork in this recipe.

1 pound lean ground beef
1 medium onion, chopped
1 clove garlic, halved
1 teaspoon curry powder
1 medium zucchini, diced
1/2 cup water
1 teaspoon salt
1/2 teaspoon sugar
1/2 teaspoon pepper
1 medium tomato, diced
1 9-ounce package pita buns, halved

In large skillet, brown meat and drain. Add onion, garlic, curry powder, zucchini, water, salt, sugar and pepper. Heat to boiling. Reduce heat, cover and simmer 15 minutes. Remove garlic halves. Stir in tomato and heat through. Just before serving, heat pita halves in microwave between layers of moist paper towels 15-20 seconds. Spoon meat mixture into pockets. Excellent with side of rice or coleslaw. Serves 8.

Per serving: 232 calories; 10.2 fat grams

Foot Notes

Adding vegetables after meat has been cooked and drained reduces the absorption of grease from the meat.

It is important to allow sliced garlic to rest 10-15 minutes before heating to allow the release of cancer-fighting compounds while cooking.

Sandwiches

TOMATO BASIL SQUARES

Heidi, Cyndi's daughter, makes this as an hors d'oeuvres. It's great as a tasty side 'wich'.

1 tube pizza dough
2 cups mozzarella cheese, shredded
2 large tomatoes, thinly sliced
2/3 cup light mayonnaise
1 clove garlic, crushed
2 tablespoons fresh basil, minced, or 2 teaspoons dry basil
1/2 cup fresh Parmesan cheese, grated

Preheat oven to 375°. Spray cookie sheet. Roll out pizza dough right on cookie sheet. Sprinkle 1 cup mozzarella cheese over dough. Arrange tomatoes over cheese. In medium bowl, mix 1 cup mozzarella cheese, mayonnaise, garlic, basil and Parmesan cheese together. Spread over tomatoes. Bake 15-20 minutes. Cut with pizza cutter. Serves 6-8.

Per serving: 256 calories; 13.5 fat grams

 Parmesan cheese is made from cow's milk and is hard and crumbly. Of course, you can buy grated Parmesan cheese at the deli, but if you choose to grate your own, use the smallest holes of a grater. The object is to create pieces of cheese that are small enough to melt readily when used in a recipe.

CROISSANT CHICKEN SALAD SANDWICH

Georgie first had a sandwich similar to this at a popular restaurant in Fort Collins, Colorado.

1 1/2 cups cooked chicken breasts, diced
1/2 cup celery, chopped
1/2 cup green grapes, halved
1/4 cup light mayonnaise
3/4 cup light whipped topping
1 4-ounce carton soft cream cheese
4 medium croissants
1/2 cup salted cashew halves
4 pieces leaf lettuce

In large bowl, combine chicken, celery and green grapes. In small bowl, combine mayonnaise and whipped topping. Mix into chicken. Spread cream cheese on bottom half of croissant. Scatter cashew halves over cream cheese. Spoon chicken mixture over cashews. Top with lettuce leaf and cover with top of croissant. Serves 4.

Per serving: 569 calories; 32.9 fat grams

 Foot Note Omit grapes and add 2 tablespoons sliced pimiento-stuffed olives to chicken salad. Serve in a hollowed out cantaloupe half that has been flattened on bottom. Serve on individual plates with green grape clusters and muffins.

OPEN FACE TUNA MELT

Salmon can be interchanged with tuna in this recipe.

2 6-ounce cans light, chunky tuna in water
1/4 cup light mayonnaise
1/2 cup celery, chopped
2-3 tablespoons onion, chopped
2-3 tablespoons green pepper, chopped
2-3 tablespoons sweet or dill pickle relish
4 English muffins, split
4 slices Swiss, dilled Havarti or Monterey
    Jack cheese
1 tomato, sliced

Spray baking sheet. In large bowl, combine tuna, mayonnaise, celery, onion, green pepper and relish. Spread evenly on English muffins. Top each with slice of cheese and tomato slice. Place on baking sheet. Set oven to broil. Heat muffins under broiler until cheese is melted. Serve with side of fresh fruit on lettuce bed. Serves 4.

Per serving: 374 calories; 10.4 fat grams

Foot Notes If you choose to serve this cold, toast English muffin before spreading with tuna salad.

Tuna Burgers are a Patrick favorite served with tomato soup on those cold winter days. Combine 2 cans drained tuna, 1/4 cup salad dressing, 1 tablespoon minced onion and 3 tablespoons sweet pickle relish. Mix well. Spread on bottom half of hamburger buns. Top each with slice of American cheese and other half of hamburger bun. Wrap in foil and heat 30 minutes in 325° oven.

OPEN-FACE RUEBENS

Ruebens are Cyndi's mom's favorite sandwich, but almost exclusively at a favorite eatery in Greeley. This one is similar without all the bread (Cyndi's favorite part!)

4 teaspoons butter or margarine
4 slices dark rye bread
1/2 cup light Thousand Island dressing
1 15-ounce can sauerkraut, well drained
8 slices corned beef
4 slices Swiss cheese

Butter bread on one side and place in large skillet over medium heat or on heated griddle. Spread dressing on unbuttered side of bread. Layer sauerkraut, corned beef and cheese. Heat until bread is nicely browned. Set oven to broil. Place skillet under broiler 5 minutes, until cheese is melted, being careful not to burn. Serves 4.

Per serving: 403 calories; 24.4 fat grams

This sandwich can be made on a rye kaiser roll as well. Heat for short period in microwave. Keep in mind that microwaving bread too long will cause it to be tough and dry.

CHICKEN CRESCENT SQUARES

Make extra crescent squares and freeze for a QUICK meal.

1 3-ounce package light cream cheese, softened
3 tablespoons margarine, melted
2 cups cooked chicken, cubed
1/4 teaspoon salt
1/2 teaspoon pepper
2 tablespoons milk
1 tablespoon chives or onion
1 tablespoon pimiento
1 8-ounce can refrigerated crescent rolls
3/4 cup seasoned croutons, crushed

Preheat oven to 350°. In large bowl, blend cream cheese and 2 tablespoons margarine. Add chicken, salt, pepper, milk, chives and pimiento; mix well. Separate crescent dough into 4 rectangles. Firmly press perforations to seal. Spoon 1/2 cup meat mixture into center of each. Pull 4 corners of dough to top center of each rectangle. Twist and seal edges. Brush with 1 tablespoon margarine. Sprinkle with crouton crumbs. Place on ungreased cookie sheet. Bake 20-25 minutes. Serves 4.

Per serving: 497 calories; 29.0 fat grams

 To make crouton crumbs, whirl croutons in blender or food processor for a minute or two.

CHICKEN QUESADILLAS

Serve as an easy lunch/snack time 'sandwich' or hors d'oeuvres.

6 6-inch flour tortillas
1 12-ounce package Monterey Jack cheese,
    cut into thin slices
2 cups cooked chicken, shredded
1 4-ounce can green chiles
2 green onions, chopped

Preheat oven to 425°. Spray 2 cookie sheets. Place tortillas on cookie sheets. Arrange cheese slices over half of each tortilla. In medium bowl, mix chicken, chiles and onions together. Spoon and spread over cheese. Fold tortillas in half. Bake 5-10 minutes until lightly browned and cheese is bubbly. Garnish with sour cream, guacamole and diced avocado. Place shredded lettuce and diced tomato on the side of tortilla. Offer salsa. Serves 6.

Per serving: 427 calories; 21.9 fat grams

 Roast fresh chiles by washing, drying and placing on a large sprayed baking sheet. Set oven to 450°. Watching carefully, roast until skins are slightly browned. Turn chiles and slightly brown other side. Remove and cool. Using rubber gloves, peel off skin. Place in zippered freezer bag and freeze.

SWISS AND SPINACH CALZONE

Make this delicious Italian treat at home and be the most popular person at the dinner table.

2 10-ounce package frozen chopped
   spinach, cooked and drained
2 cups Swiss cheese, shredded
3/4 cup green onions, finely chopped
1 teaspoon dried basil, crushed
2 cloves garlic, minced
2 12-ounce packages refrigerator rolls

Preheat oven to 400°. Spray large cookie sheet. In large bowl, stir together spinach, cheese, onions, basil and garlic. Knead 2 rolls together and place on cookie sheet. Roll and stretch to at least twice their size. Spoon filling mixture onto one side of each roll. Fold other side over filling to form half-moon shape. Press edges to seal and flute with fork impressions. Bake 10-12 minutes. Serve with salad. Serves 8.

Per serving: 348 calories; 12.0 fat grams

 Test your creativity and make some of our favorite fillings. We suggest: ham, pineapple, cream cheese and green onion; Italian sausage, pasta sauce and mozzarella cheese; or green peppers, onions, mushrooms and alfredo pasta sauce. Have fun!!

Sandwiches

HAM AND SWISS TORTILLA WRAP

Georgie's bridge group members lay out quite a spread for an evening of fun. Georgie served a variety of wraps that just had to be included.

2 tablespoons cream cheese and pineapple
    spread
1 large flour tortilla
1 tablespoon salad dressing
1 tablespoon dijon mustard
2 slices deli honey baked ham
2 slices swiss cheese
1/4 cup alfalfa sprouts
Lettuce leaves

Spread cream cheese on tortilla. In small bowl, mix salad dressing and mustard. Spread thin layer over cream cheese. Layer remaining ingredients in order given. Leaving ends open, roll up tightly from one side. Slice diagonally into 3-4 pieces. Place on serving dish, seam side down. Serves 2.

Per Serving: 320 calories; 21.8 fat grams

 Foot Notes Make a variety of wraps using different flavored tortillas. Arrange on large platter covered with bed of lettuce leaves.

The secret to a good wrap is something spreadable and a combination of your favorite ingredients. It's a convenient way to serve meals while camping or boating.

VEGGIES ON TOMATO WRAP

"It's always a challenge to come up with new ideas for bridge," says Georgie. "These tortilla wraps were QUICK, easy and a big hit."

2 tablespoons garden-flavored cream cheese
    spread
1 sun-dried tomato flavored tortilla wrap
3-4 fresh mushrooms, sliced
1/4 green pepper, sliced
1/4 red pepper, sliced
1/4 yellow pepper, sliced
1 green onion, chopped
Lettuce leaves
1/4 cup alfalfa sprouts
3-4 black olives sliced

Spread cream cheese on tortilla. Layer remaining ingredients in order given. Leaving ends open, roll tightly. Slice diagonally into 3-4 pieces and place on serving dish, seam side down. Serves 2.

Per serving: 399 calories; 16.3 fat grams

Foot Notes

Try this one warm. Sauté vegetables including olives. Serve shredded lettuce and sprouts with slices of tomatoes on the side.

Tortilla wraps are larger and thinner than the regular variety and come in many flavors.

TURKEY ON SPINACH WRAP

Georgie's love of cashews with chicken or turkey was the inspiration behind this wrap.

2 tablespoons cream cheese spread
2 tablespoons ranch dressing
1 large spinach flavored tortilla wrap
1/4 cup cashews, broken
2-3 slices deli roast turkey
Spinach or lettuce leaves
1/4 cup alfalfa sprouts

Spread cream cheese and ranch dressing on tortilla. Press cashews into cream cheese. Layer turkey, spinach and sprouts. Leaving ends open, roll up gently, but tightly. Place on serving plate, seam side down. Serves 2.

Per serving: 433 calories; 18.6 fat grams

Foot Notes

For a refreshing change, add Havarti dill cheese or a flavored cream cheese. Substitute roast beef and cheddar for the turkey.

For an attractive presentation, place potato or pasta salad in center of a large platter with tortilla wraps and veggies arranged around the outside.

CHICKEN CAESAR WRAP

M-m-m good! If you like Caesar salad, you're going to love this wrap.

1 10-ounce package Caesar Romaine salad mix
2 large skinless chicken breast halves, cooked and cut into strips
4 medium tomatoes, chopped
2 tablespoons green onion, chopped
6 tablespoons Caesar salad dressing
6 large tortillas, any flavor, at room temperature
2 tablespoons Parmesan cheese
Salt and pepper to taste

In large bowl, combine salad mix, chicken, tomatoes and green onion. Toss with salad dressing. Place 2 cups salad down center of each tortilla. Sprinkle each salad with 1 teaspoon Parmesan cheese, salt and pepper. Fold bottom of tortilla up over salad and fold both sides to center overlapping slightly. Secure with toothpicks. Serves 6.

Per serving: 289 calories; 14.9 fat grams

Foot Note A lighter version without raw eggs:

Mock Caesar Salad Dressing
1/4 cup fresh lemon juice
1/4 cup red wine vinegar
3/4 cup olive oil
Garlic salt to taste
Pepper to taste
Dash Worcestershire sauce
1/4 cup light blue cheese dressing
Combine all ingredients in container with lid and shake until well mixed.

MINI PIZZAS

Use these QUICK and easy miniature pizzas as a side to eggs or salads or as hors d'oeuvres.

8 ounces pre-made pizza dough
7 tablespoons butter, softened
1 tablespoon green onions, finely chopped
1 tablespoon fresh oregano, finely chopped
1/2 teaspoon lemon juice
1/2 teaspoon grated lemon peel
2 plum tomatoes, sliced crosswise
6 marinated artichokes, finely chopped
10 fresh mushrooms, finely chopped
8 stuffed green olives, sliced
4 ounces mozzarella cheese
8 pitted black olives
16 basil leaves

Preheat oven to 400°. Generously spray 9 x 13-inch baking sheet. Slice pizza dough into 8 3/4-inch pieces. On floured surface, roll each dough slice to about 4" in diameter. Place on baking sheet. In small dish, combine onions, oregano, lemon juice and lemon peel. Spread on each pizza round. In medium bowl, combine tomatoes, artichokes, mushrooms and green olives. Spoon onto rounds. Top with slices of mozzarella cheese. Bake 15-20 minutes. Garnish with black olives and basil leaves. Serves 8.

Per serving: 261 calories; 17.1 fat grams

To freeze fresh basil, trim stems, wash and chop. Place 1 tablespoon in each compartment of an ice cube tray. Pour boiling water to cover and freeze. Unmold into freezer bag, freeze and keep up to 4 months. The theory behind the boiling water is blanching. This method can be used on other tender leaf herbs.

Pizza

SHISH KABOBS WITH GEORGIE'S MARINADE

No, 'kabob' isn't spelled wrong; it can also be spelled 'kebab'. QUICK, but you'll need to prepare meat early in the day. We included the Patricks' favorite things to skewer. Make your own signature kabob.

1/4 cup soy sauce
3 tablespoons honey
2 tablespoons red wine vinegar
1 onion, chopped
1/2 teaspoon garlic salt
1 1/2 teaspoons ginger
3/4 cup oil
1 1/2 pounds round or sirloin steak, or
    chicken cut in 1 1/2-inch cubes, or
    whole shrimp
1 medium red or green bell pepper, cut into
    1-inch pieces
1 small onion, cut into 1-inch pieces
12 small button mushrooms
1/2 cup pineapple chunks

In blender, whirl soy sauce, honey, wine vinegar, onion, garlic salt, ginger and oil until well blended and thickened. Pour marinade over meat in a 9 x 13-inch dish. Cover and refrigerate 4-6 hours or overnight. Preheat grill. Thread beef and vegetables, alternating items onto 8 9-inch skewers. Cook on grill until meat is done to each individual taste. Serves 8.

Per serving: 491 calories; 37.7 fat grams

 Foot Notes

If using potatoes, place potatoes in microwavable dish, cover with vented plastic wrap and microwave on high 4-7 minutes, until potatoes are barely tender.

For QUICKer recipe, with no marinating time, use Italian or Caesar-type dressing to toss with all ingredients.

Kabobs

SHRIMP SCAMPI KABOBS

A delicious and impressive treat for shrimp lovers.

21-26 peeled shrimp
3/4 teaspoon salt
1/2 teaspoon oregano
1/2 teaspoon thyme leaves
1/4 cup butter or margarine
4 cloves garlic, minced
1 tablespoon parsley
12 whole fresh mushrooms
12 cherry tomatoes

Toss shrimp with salt, oregano and thyme. Chill 30 minutes. Preheat oven to 375°. Melt butter; add garlic and parsley. Set aside. Thread 3 shrimp on each of 8 skewers, spacing with cherry tomato and a mushroom. Place in baking pan and brush each kabob with garlic butter being especially generous on the mushrooms. Bake 12-15 minutes being careful not to overcook. Serve on rice pilaf with salad. Serves 4.

Per serving: 247 calories; 13.5 fat grams

Foot Note Marinade shrimp in prepared teriyaki sauce and skewer with green pepper and pineapple chunks. Serve with 'sticky' rice.

Kabobs

BLACK BEAN TORTILLA PIE

Hardly any preparation time goes into this recipe. The results are showy and QUICK.

1 11-ounce jar medium salsa
1 8-ounce can no-salt-added tomato sauce
1 15-ounce can black beans, rinsed and
    drained
1 15-ounce can whole-kernel corn, drained
1/2 cup fresh cilantro leaves
4 10-inch lowfat flour tortillas
1 1/2 cups reduced-fat Monterey Jack
    cheese, shredded
1/2 cup light sour cream

Preheat oven to 500°. Spray 10 x 15-inch pan. In small bowl, mix salsa and tomato sauce. In medium bowl, mix black beans, corn and cilantro. Place 1 tortilla in pan. Spread with 1/3 of salsa mixture. Top with 1/3 bean mixture and 1/3 cheese. Spread next tortilla with 1/3 sour cream and place spread side down on top of cheese. Repeat 2 more times, ending with last tortilla. Bake 10-12 minutes, until edges of tortillas are browned. Watch carefully. Cut into 6 wedges. Serve with side of lettuce wedge and favorite salad dressing. Serves 6.

Per serving: 445 calories; 18.5 fat grams

Prolong life of cilantro by trimming stems, placing stem side down in jar of water and covering with plastic wrap. Cilantro will stay fresh up to a month in the refrigerator.

FAJITA CASSEROLE

The original fajitas are pretty QUICK, but this is a fun, fix-and-forget dish created by Cyndi for a QUICK meal when there are a lot of other things to be done before guests arrive.

6 large flour tortillas (corn tortillas can also be used, if preferred)
2 cups Monterey Jack cheese, shredded
2 tablespoons olive oil
1 large onion, sliced and separated into rings
1 green pepper, sliced into strips
1/2 red pepper, sliced into strips
1/2 yellow pepper, sliced into strips
1-2 cloves garlic, chopped
1 envelope taco seasoning mix
2 cups light sour cream
3 tablespoons light mayonnaise
1 tablespoon lime juice
3 chicken breasts, cooked, shredded or cut into pieces
1 cup salsa
1 cup cheddar cheese, shredded

Preheat oven to 350°. Spray large 10 x 15-inch casserole dish. Place two tortillas on bottom. Spread with Monterey Jack cheese. In large skillet, heat oil and sauté onion, peppers and garlic. Spread over tortillas and cheese. Place two more tortillas on top of peppers. In medium bowl, stir taco mix, sour cream, mayonnaise and lime juice together. Spread on tortillas. Cover with chicken pieces. Top with last two tortillas. Spread with salsa and sprinkle with cheddar cheese. Bake 30-40 minutes. Serves 8.

Per serving: 388 calories; 22.5 fat grams

 Use the same procedure with beef, or omit the meat and make it vegetarian.

MEXICAN CHICKEN

Georgie's friend, Nancy, shared this recipe as an easy way to use leftover chicken or turkey.

3 cups cooked chicken breast, cut up
1 onion, chopped
1 tablespoon oil
2 4-ounce cans diced green chiles
1 10-ounce can cream of chicken soup
1 10-ounce can cream of celery soup
1 cup chicken broth
1 cup milk
2 cups Monterey Jack cheese, shredded
1 cup sharp cheddar cheese, shredded
1 package flour tortillas

Preheat oven to 350°. Spray 9 x 13-inch casserole dish. In large pan, sauté onion in oil. Add green chiles, soups, broth and milk. Put a layer of tortillas in bottom of casserole dish. Spoon half of soup mixture on top of tortillas. Sprinkle with 1/2 the chicken. Spread 1/2 the cheeses on top of chicken. repeat layers ending with cheese. Bake uncovered 35-40 minutes, until hot. Serves 8-10.

Per serving: 414 calories; 20.7 fat grams

 Soy, half & half, skim or lowfat milk can be substituted for the milk. Use your favorite soup combinations.

Casseroles

WESTERN TURKEY CASSEROLE

Georgie writes recipes on the craziest things: napkins, bridge score pads, bank receipts, etc. This one is on a magazine subscription card. Where could she have been?

1 pound turkey breast, cut into strips
1 small onion, chopped
2 tablespoons oil
1 cup taco sauce
2 cups shredded Monterey Jack cheese
1/4 cup flour
4 large eggs, beaten
3/4 cup milk
2 7-ounce cans whole green chiles

Preheat oven to 350°. Spray 8 x 10-inch baking dish. In large skillet, cook turkey and onion in oil 5 minutes. Add taco sauce. Lower heat to keep warm. In medium bowl, toss cheese and flour. Beat eggs and milk; add to cheese and mix well. Slice chiles open and rinse. Layer 1/2 the chiles, 1/2 the turkey and 1/2 the cheese mixture, then repeat. Bake uncovered 40 minutes. Let stand 5 minutes to set. Serves 6.

Per serving: 408 calories; 26.3 fat grams

 Foot Notes Fresh turkey or chicken breasts are more easily and evenly cut when partially frozen.

Deviate from the casserole presentation by cooking extra large pasta shells. Mix all ingredients, except cheese. Stuff shells. Place in sprayed 9 x 13-inch baking dish; top with cheese and bake 30 minutes at 350°.

CHICKEN OR TURKEY CASSEROLE

Leftover chicken or Thanksgiving turkey won't go to waste with recipes like this at your fingertips.

2 cups chicken or turkey, cooked and shred-
    ded or cubed
1/2 cup slivered almonds, toasted
1 8-ounce can water chestnuts, sliced
2 teaspoons lemon juice
1/2 cup fresh mushrooms, sliced
1/2 teaspoon salt
1 cup light mayonnaise
1/2 cup cheddar cheese, shredded
1/2 cup French fried onions

Preheat oven to 350°. Spray 8 x 10-inch dish. In large bowl, mix all ingredients, except cheese and onions. Pour into dish. Top with cheese and onions. Bake 30-40 minutes. Serves 8.

Per serving: 367 calories; 24.2 fat grams

 French fried onions are the delicious topping for the famous green bean casserole found on so many holiday tables.

Reduce preparation time by remembering to buy water chestnuts and mushrooms already sliced, cheese shredded and lemons juiced. (Georgie couldn't resist, but it's a fact; we Cyndi's should take it to heart!)

PASTA CRUSTED BEEF PIE

Guess what this recipe is written on. . .a computer paper with a spelling list from Georgie's teaching days. Don't you love it? How many of you write recipes down like this?

2 cups spaghetti, cooked (leftover is good)
2 tablespoons butter, melted
1/3 cup Parmesan cheese
2 eggs, beaten
1 cup lowfat cottage cheese
1 pound lean ground beef
1/2 cup onion, chopped
1/2 cup green pepper, chopped
1 8-ounce can stewed tomatoes, cut up
1 6-ounce can tomato paste
1 teaspoon sugar
1 teaspoon oregano
1/2 teaspoon garlic salt
2/3 cup mozzarella cheese, shredded

Preheat oven to 350°. Spray deep-dish pie plate. In large bowl, mix hot spaghetti and butter together. Add Parmesan cheese and eggs. Form crust in dish. Spoon cottage cheese over crust. In large skillet, brown beef and drain. Add onion, green pepper tomatoes, tomato paste, sugar, oregano and garlic salt. Pour over crust. Bake, uncovered, 20 minutes. Sprinkle cheese over top and bake 5 minutes more. Serves 6.

Per serving: 468 calories; 23.8 fat grams

The life of cottage cheese can be prolonged by turning the carton upside down in refrigerator after opening.

Yes, you can freeze cooked pasta. Reheat in microwave or pasta sauce.

Casseroles

CREAMY CHICKEN BREASTS

The 'gravy' in this very popular dish is wonderful with rice, potatoes AND vegetables. If you should have some left over, cut up the chicken and mix with gravy, add cut up vegetables and make a pot pie.

1 10-ounce can cream of mushroom soup
1 4-ounce can of sliced mushrooms
1 cup light sour cream
1/2 cup sherry
4 whole (8 halves) chicken breasts, boned, skinned
Paprika
1 1/2 cups lowfat cheddar cheese, shredded

Preheat oven to 350°. Spray 9 x 13-inch baking dish. In large bowl, mix soup, mushrooms, sour cream and sherry. Place chicken breasts in baking dish. Pour soup mixture over chicken. Sprinkle generously with paprika. Bake 1 1/2 hours. Serve with rice and fresh vegetables. Serves 6-8.

Per serving: 460 calories; 9.6 fat grams

If you like to fix one-pot meals, put carrots and/or green beans on bottom of baking dish before placing chicken in dish.

If you don't have sherry use 1 tablespoon Worcestershire sauce and enough water to make 1/2 cup.

SHRIMP STUFFED POTATOES

There are so many ways to stuff potatoes for QUICK lunches or dinner. This one is wonderful with or without the shrimp.

4 medium baking potatoes
1/4 cup butter or margarine
1/4 cup half & half or lowfat milk
4 teaspoons green onion, chopped
1 cup sharp cheddar, shredded
1 teaspoon salt
1 pound shrimp, cooked and peeled
Paprika
Parsley

Preheat oven to 425°. Scrub potatoes thoroughly. Bake 40-60 minutes. (We would pierce each potato in several places and microwave them on high 4 minutes. Turn and microwave on high 2 minutes. Place in oven and bake 10-15 minutes to crisp skin.) Cool slightly. Using clean oven mitt, cut potatoes in half lengthwise. Carefully scoop out pulp leaving shell about 1/4-inch thick. Combine potato pulp, butter and half & half. Beat or mash until smooth. Stir in onion, cheese, salt and shrimp. Stuff shells with potato mixture. Sprinkle with paprika and parsley. Heat in oven 15 minutes or microwave on high 1-2 minutes. Serves 4.

Per serving: 408 calories; 22.9 fat grams

Foot Note Other combinations: slit top of potato and squeeze to loosen pulp (no need to scoop out). Top with leftover chili, onions and cheese; cooked broccoli, onions and melted processed cheese; asparagus, ham and melted white cheddar; or traditional butter, sour cream, chives and bacon bits.

HOT CRAB BOATS

These would be fun served at a luncheon with a nautical theme. Decorate them with little sails made of toothpicks and paper.

6 French rolls
1/2 cup butter, melted
1 1/2 cups crabmeat
3/4 cup celery, diced
3/4 cup frozen peas, thawed
3/4 pound Swiss cheese, cubed
3 tablespoons parsley
1/2 cup light sour cream
2 teaspoons lemon juice
3/4 teaspoon seasoned salt
Dash pepper

Preheat oven to 400°. Spray large baking pan. Cut thin slice from top of each roll. Scoop out soft interior. Brush inside of shells with melted butter. In large bowl, combine remaining ingredients. Fill shells. Place on baking pan. Bake 15 minutes. Serve hot. Serves 6.

Per serving: 440 calories; 28.1 fat grams

 To make croutons or bread crumbs from rolls or stale bread, cube and place in microwavable dish. For croutons, toss bread in mixture of olive oil and favorite seasonings. Microwave on high two minutes. Turn bread cubes. Microwave at 1 minutes intervals, turning in between, until dry and lightly browned. To make crumbs, whirl croutons in blender or food processor until fine.

Omit the French rolls and serve cold on croissants or as a stuffed tomato. Shred the cheese.

SALMON CAKES

This recipe calls for salmon, but you can use crab, tuna, shrimp or canned chicken. Our moms served salmon 'patties' as a main dish for a Quick meal.

1 14-ounce can red or pink salmon, drained
    and flaked
1 green onion, sliced
3 tablespoons prepared horseradish sauce,
    or plain yogurt
2 tablespoons plain bread crumbs
1 teaspoon soy sauce
1/4 teaspoon fresh coarsely ground pepper
1 teaspoon oil
4 sandwich buns, split
Lettuce leaves

In medium bowl, lightly mix salmon, onion, horseradish, bread crumbs, soy sauce and pepper with fork. Shape into 4 patties. Spray large skillet, add oil and cook patties 5 minutes on each side, browning until golden. Serve on buns with lettuce and condiments. Serves 4.

Per serving: 317 calories; 8.4 fat grams

Foot Note

Plain yogurt can be substituted for oil and butter in recipes. To reduce calories in this recipe, mix plain yogurt with plain horseradish, instead of using the prepared horseradish sauce.

CRISPY SALMON FILETS

The Duncans have salmon for lunches or 'dunches', a term coined by the siblings for an early supper served between lunch and dinner.

1/4 cup butter or margarine
2/3 cup fresh bread crumbs or crushed
    saltines
1/4 cup grated Parmesan cheese
1/2 teaspoon dried basil (Cyndi uses fresh
    when available from the garden)
1/2 teaspoon oregano
1/4 teaspoon garlic salt
4 6-ounce salmon filets (use larger ones if
    serving for dinner)

Preheat oven to 350°. In microwave, melt butter in shallow dish. Mix in bread crumbs, Parmesan cheese, basil, oregano and garlic salt. Dip salmon into butter, then coat both sides with crumb mixture. Place in baking dish. Bake, uncovered, 30-35 minutes. Salmon will flake easily. Serves 4.

Per serving: 332 calories; 18.9 fat grams

Fresh bread crumbs will make a crispier coating than dried bread crumbs or crackers.

PICNIC LUNCH IN A FOIL PACKET

The Patrick family made these individual packets to cook in the campfire coals. Everyone built their own from a selection of favorite ingredients-no zucchini for Bob. The Duncans took theirs already assembled.

1 pound beef round steak, 4 chicken breast halves or 4 lean ground beef patties
1 16-ounce package frozen peas and carrots, or mixed vegetables, partially thawed
2 medium potatoes, peeled and sliced
1 10-ounce can cream of mushroom soup, or other soup of choice
1 envelope onion soup mix
8 cherry tomatoes, optional

Heat oven or grill to 450°. Make 4 packets from 18 x 15-inch pieces of heavy duty foil. Cut meat or chicken into 1-inch pieces; leave hamburger as patty. In small bowl, mix soups together. Place meat evenly into packets. Top with vegetables. Spoon soup mixture over meat and peas. Wrap foil around meat and vegetables securely. Place on ungreased baking sheet. Bake 35-40 minutes. Garnish with cherry tomatoes. Serves 4.

Per serving: 403 calories; 17.3 fat grams

 Foot Notes Fix ahead and freeze. Thaw at room temperature. Baking time will be longer if partially frozen.

Add sliced onions and use condensed tomato soup in place of soup mixture.

FRESH VEGGIE PASTA

This is a QUICK and easy way to use extra fresh vegetables from the garden or Farmers' Market. Preparation time is last minute, so have all sides on the table when pasta dish is ready to serve.

3 tablespoons olive oil
1 onion, sliced and broken into rings
1 cup broccoli, broken into florets
2 cups red, yellow and green peppers (use only green pepper, if preferred)
1 cup mushrooms, sliced
1/2 cup carrots, cut into 2 x 1/4-inch strips
1-2 cloves garlic, minced
1 teaspoon oregano
2 tablespoons fresh basil, chopped
4 cups cooked pasta-rotini, fettuccini, spiral, penne
2 teaspoons chicken bouillon granules
1/2 cup lowfat milk or cream
1/2 cup Parmesan cheese
Salt and ground pepper to taste

In large wok or skillet, heat oil. Sauté all vegetables and garlic 8-10 minutes. Add oregano, basil, pasta, bouillon and milk. Simmer 5 minutes. The sauce will thicken quickly. Stir in Parmesan cheese, salt and pepper. Serve immediately in a large pasta dish or as individual servings. Great with garlic bread or breadsticks. Serves 4-6.

Per serving: 316 calories, 12.1 fat grams

Foot Note
Other combinations: 2 cups cut-up asparagus, 1 cup diagonally sliced celery, 1 cup cut up ham and 1 cup sliced red pepper; or sliced onion, celery, carrots and frozen peas, topped with halved cherry tomatoes. Use same sauce, prepared pasta sauce or create your own. Throw some leftover chicken, shrimp or bacon into any of these combinations.

HOT LEFTOVER PASTA SALAD PLUS

Tired of the pasta salad served at Sunday's picnic, but there's too much to throw away? Well, use it up! Leftovers never looked so good.

3 tablespoons olive oil
8 spears asparagus, cut into bite-size pieces
2-3 cups broccoli and red, green or yellow
    peppers
4 green onions, sliced in 2-inch pieces
2 cups cooked chicken, sliced or shredded
2-3 cups pasta salad (this usually has some
    veggies, olives and dressing in it)
1/2 teaspoon garlic salt
1/2 teaspoon granulated garlic
1/4 cup light Italian dressing
1 tomato, quartered and sliced

In large skillet heat oil. Sauté asparagus and vegetables 5 minutes. Add chicken, pasta salad, garlic seasonings and dressing; heat through. Add tomato. Serve immediately. Serves 6.

Per serving: 434 calories; 33.0 fat grams
(varies depending on pasta salad used)

Foot Note Make a pasta pie by spreading pasta salad into sprayed deep-dish pie pan. Spread remaining ingredients on top and cover with mozzarella cheese. Bake 30 minutes at 350°.

MAPLE CHICKEN SALAD

Another unusual recipe similar to one at Andy's Restaurant in Gatesville, Texas, where Georgie's mom cooks. If you were tasting this salad for the secret ingredient, would you have guessed maple syrup?

4 chicken breasts, cooked and diced
1 cup seedless green or red grapes, halved
1 stalk celery, diced
1/2 cup pecan pieces
3/4 cup salad dressing (not mayonnaise)
3 tablespoons maple syrup

In large bowl, toss first four ingredients together. In small bowl, combine salad dressing and maple syrup. Pour over chicken mixture and mix well. Divide onto lettuce cups or use as filling for stuffed tomatoes. Garnish plate with slices of cantaloupe and grape clusters. Serves 4-5.

Per serving: 349 calories; 19.4 fat grams

Foot Note To cook chicken in microwave, place chicken breasts in microwavable baking dish, thickest parts closest to outside of the dish. Add 2-3 tablespoons water or chicken broth. Cover with plastic wrap vented on one corner and microwave on high 5 minutes. Allow to stand another 5 minutes to finish cooking. Test for doneness. Turn chicken and repeat at shorter intervals, if needed, to complete cooking. It gets tough if cooked too long.

Salads

HOT CHICKEN SALAD

This tasty salad was served at a shower for Georgie when she was expecting Toni. It was also served to Cyndi at a luncheon given by Heidi's piano teacher.

2 cups chicken, cooked and cubed
2 cups instant rice
1/2 cup slivered almonds
1 1/2 cups celery, diced
1 tablespoon dry minced onion
4 hard-cooked eggs, chopped
2 tablespoons lemon juice
1 10-ounce can cream of chicken soup
1 10-ounce can cream of mushroom soup
1 cup American processed cheese, cubed
1 cup light mayonnaise or salad dressing
2 8-ounce cans water chestnuts, chopped,
    optional
1 cup green olives with pimientos, sliced,
    optional (not a choice of Georgie's)
1/2 teaspoon freshly ground pepper
1 cup crushed potato chips

In large bowl, mix all ingredients together, except potato chips. Pour into 9 x 13-inch baking dish. Refrigerate several hours or overnight. Preheat oven to 350°. Sprinkle potato chips on top. Bake, uncovered, 45-60 minutes. Serves 12-14.

Per serving: 343 calories; 17.9 fat grams

Great served with a tossed salad, hot bread and fruit or light dessert.

Salads

TUNA SALAD WITH A SURPRISE

The horseradish flavor adds an unusual zest to a favorite lunch time salad. Serve as a sandwich, stuffed tomato or hot open-face sandwich with melted Swiss cheese.

2 6-ounce cans white albacore tuna, drained
3 stalks celery, sliced
1/2 cup onion, chopped
1/4 cup sweet pickle relish
1/2 cup light mayonnaise or salad dressing
3-4 tablespoons pub style horseradish sauce
    (found in the deli)
1/4 cup walnuts, coarsely chopped, or sun-
    flower seed kernels, optional

In large bowl, mix all ingredients together. Serve on bed of lettuce leaves. Serves 4.

Per serving: 231 calories; 9.6 fat grams

 Substitute salmon to make an elegant salad. Try adding cucumbers to tuna or salmon.

Replacing horseradish sauce with dijon mustard, adds a whole new dimension to this salad.

SWEET AND SOUR SPINACH SALAD

The 4 'S' salad. We both have used this recipe, made adjustments to it, and served it often.

4-6 generous cups of spinach, washed and
    drained
1/2 cup bacon, fried crisp, broken
4 hard-cooked eggs, sliced or grated
1/2 red onion, sliced and broken into rings
1/2 cup fresh mushrooms, sliced

Sweet and Sour Dressing-this recipe
    makes enough for two or three salads
    depending on how much you prefer to
    use.
1 cup oil
1/3 cup red wine vinegar
1/4 cup light mayonnaise
1/4 cup chili sauce
1/4 teaspoon salt
2 tablespoons sugar
Pinch cayenne pepper
1/4 teaspoon garlic powder

In large salad bowl, mix all salad ingredients. Just before serving, pour desired amount of dressing over salad and toss. Serves 4.

Sweet and Sour Dressing
Put all ingredients into shaker jar and shake to mix well. Refrigerate until ready to use. Shake again before serving.

Per serving: 429 calories; 37.7 fat grams

Add other ingredients like cucumber or mandarin oranges to this salad.

Salads

STRAWBERRY SPINACH TOSS

The lemon honey dressing on this salad adds just the right 'bite'.

1 large head red leaf lettuce
1 10-ounce package fresh spinach
1 cup pecan halves, toasted
1/2 pound fresh mushrooms, sliced
1 pint fresh strawberries, washed, stemmed
    and sliced lengthwise
1/2 medium red onion, thinly sliced

Lemon-Honey Dressing
2 tablespoons honey
2 tablespoons dijon mustard
1 teaspoon grated lemon peel
1/2 cup fresh lemon juice
1/2 cup olive oil
1/2 cup salad oil
Fresh ground pepper, optional

Place all salad ingredients in large salad bowl.
Cover with damp towel and refrigerate. Shake salad
dressing and pour over salad just before serving or
offer on the side. Serves 8.

Lemon-Honey Dressing
Place all dressing ingredients in blender and whirl
until thick and creamy.

Per serving: 345 calories; 32.6 fat grams

In the winter when strawberries aren't
at their best, substitute pomegranate
seeds, dried cranberries, dried cherries or mandarin oranges.

TOMATO AND FRESH MOZZARELLA SALAD

Our friend, Cheryl, serves this QUICK, easy and delicious salad when tomatoes are plentiful; it is always a hit. She was served it first by her sister in California.

10 tomatoes, thinly sliced
1/2 pound fresh mozzarella cheese, thinly sliced
1 red onion, or sweet white onion, thinly sliced and broken into rings
1/2 cup black olives, thinly sliced, optional (mainly used for color contrast)
1/2 cup balsamic vinegarette salad dressing
Salt and pepper to taste
1/2 cup fresh basil leaves

On large platter, layer tomatoes, mozzarella cheese, onions and olives. Sprinkle each layer with dressing, salt, pepper and basil leaves. Serves 8-10.

Per serving: 123 calories; 7.5 fat grams

Foot Notes

Can you picture this layered in a straight-sided salad dish, or imagine it heated in a casserole dish with the addition of Parmesan cheese and broiled?

Freeze mozzarella cheese, thaw and crumble. This gives salads an entirely different appearance.

Salads

NOT TOO SPICY GAZPACHO

Do this one by committee (have each person bring an ingredient or two).

1 59-ounce bottle Bloody Mary mix
1 12-ounce can tomato juice
3 cucumbers, peeled
1 large onion
1 green pepper (you can use a large green
    chile if you prefer 'heat')
1 stalk celery
2 large tomatoes
4-6 tablespoons wine vinegar
4-6 tablespoons sugar
2 tablespoons lemon juice
2 tablespoons Worcestershire sauce
2-4 tablespoons olive or vegetable oil

In large tureen or punch bowl, combine Bloody Mary mix and tomato juice. In food processor or blender, whirl cucumbers, onion, green pepper, celery and tomatoes until as smooth as possible. Add to juice mixture, stirring to mix well. Add vinegar, sugar, lemon juice, Worcestershire sauce and oil. Stir well. Chill. Serve in frosty margarita glasses rimmed with salt or fun soup bowls with a crispy salad. Serves 12.

Per serving: 88 calories; 2.6 fat grams

Freeze any leftover gazpacho and use as a base for hot vegetable soups.

Freeze gazpacho in ice cube trays; use as 'ice cubes' in Bloody Mary drinks.

BUTTER BEAN SOUP

Enjoy a warm, colorful meatless soup.

1 onion, coarsely chopped
1 12-ounce package frozen mixed vegetables
1 15-ounce can butter beans, drained
2 16-ounce cans stewed tomatoes
1 small zucchini, quartered, sliced
2 16-ounce cans chicken broth, or 3-4 bouillon cubes and 3 cups water
1/2 teaspoon pepper
1 teaspoon dill weed
1/2 cup Parmesan cheese
Croutons, optional

In large pan, combine all ingredients, except Parmesan cheese and croutons. Simmer over low heat 25-30 minutes. Ladle into soup bowls; top with dill weed, cheese and croutons. Serves 6.

Per serving: 250 calories; 4.4 at grams

 Make it heartier by adding cooked meatballs and substituting beef broth for the chicken broth. Don't know what to do with leftover meatloaf? Put it in the soup with the beef broth base; it gives it a great flavor.

MEXICAN PORK STEW

This is a modified, QUICK version of the traditional Mexican Posole, full of meat, vegetables and flavor. Plan ahead for the soaking of chiles.

1 ounce dried New Mexico red chiles (found in Mexican food section of grocery store, usually sold in plastic or cellophane package)
3/4 cup boiling water
1 cup leftover pork roast, or 1/2 pound pork, cooked and shredded
3 cloves garlic
1 teaspoon oregano (Mexican oregano is best, but hard to find)
1 tablespoon oil
6 cups water
2 cups chicken broth
1 1/2 teaspoons salt
1/2 cup onion, chopped
1 30-ounce can white hominy (if you don't like hominy, substitute white beans), rinsed and drained

Tortilla Strips
4 corn tortillas
1/2 cup oil

In food processor, soak red chiles in boiling water while preparing rest of soup. In large pan, sauté pork, 2 cloves garlic and oregano in oil 5 minutes. Add water, chicken broth and 1 teaspoon salt. Bring to boil; reduce heat and simmer while preparing red chili mixture. Whirl red chile mixture with onion, 1 clove garlic and 1/2 teaspoon salt. Stir mixture and hominy into soup. Simmer 30 minutes. Ladle into soup bowls and top with tortilla strips. Offer diced avocado, shredded lettuce, chopped onion, shredded cheese, chopped cilantro, and/or red pepper flakes. Serves 6-8.

Tortilla Strips
Cut tortillas into short thin strips. In large high sided skillet, heat oil. Fry tortilla strips, stirring and turning, 1-2 minutes. Lift with slotted spoon onto paper towels to drain. Store, covered at room temperature 2-3 days.

Per serving: 285 calories; 14.9 fat grams

MEATBALL SOUP

Try different combinations of vegetables and pastas. This soup is different every time Georgie makes it.

3 cups beef broth
2 cups mixed vegetables, chopped, fresh or
    frozen
1 15-ounce can stewed tomatoes
18 frozen meatballs
2 bay leaves
1/2 teaspoon pepper
1 cup favorite pasta, cooked

Place first 6 ingredients in slow cooker; stir. Cook on low, 6-8 hours. Add pasta 1/2 hour before serving. Remove bay leaves and discard. Spoon into soup bowls. Serves 6.

Per serving: 251 calories; 11.5 fat grams

 Georgie finds the flavor of beef broth a little overwhelming, so she dilutes it with water or tomato juice. You'll often find her adding steak sauce, catsup or Worcestershire sauce to her soups.

GREAT NORTHERN MINESTRONE

This is really a QUICK dump soup so don't let the long list of ingredients scare you off.

1 pound Italian sausage, either bulk or link
1 tablespoon olive oil
1 onion, chopped
1 clove garlic, finely minced
1 cup carrots, sliced
1 teaspoon basil, crushed, or 2 tablespoons
    fresh basil, chopped
1 teaspoon oregano
1 bay leaf
2 small zucchini, sliced
1 28-ounce can crushed Italian tomatoes
2 10-ounce cans beef broth
1 10-ounce can chicken broth
2 cups cabbage, finely shredded
1 teaspoon salt
1/2 teaspoon pepper
2 16-ounce cans great northern beans,
    undrained
1 10-ounce package chopped frozen
    spinach, thawed and drained

In large pan, brown sausage in oil (if using link sausage, slice 1/2-inch thick and brown). Drain. Add onion, garlic, carrots, basil, oregano and bay leaf. Cook 5 minutes. Add zucchini, tomatoes, broths, cabbage, salt and pepper. Bring soup to boil; reduce heat and simmer, covered 1 hour. Add beans and spinach; cook 20 minutes. Garnish with parsley flakes. Offer good Italian bread and salad as side dishes. Serves 8-10.

Per serving: 379 calories; 19.2 fat grams

 You can omit the sausage and still have a flavorful Italian soup. Diet experts say that eating a liquid-type soup is more filling, less fattening and can result in your eating less.

This soup is better the second day after flavors have mingled. It freezes well.

VERDE BEAN SOUP

This is a recipe that the two of us enjoyed at a restaurant somewhere. We picked it apart and came up with this very flavorful soup.

3 cups V-8, or tomato juice

1 cup water

1 16-ounce can tomatoes

1 16-ounce can kidney beans, rinsed and drained

1 8-ounce can corn, drained or 1 cup frozen corn

1 8-ounce can green beans, drained or 1 cup frozen green beans

4 chicken bouillon cubes

1 4-ounce can green chiles

1 packet taco seasoning mix

4 corn tortillas, broken into pieces

In large pan, combine all ingredients, except tortillas. Bring to boil. Reduce heat and simmer 30 minutes or put in crockpot and cook on low 4-6 hours. Line 4 soup bowls with corn tortillas. Ladle soup into dishes and top with shredded white cheddar. Serves 4.

Per serving: 306 calories; 2.6 fat grams

 When heating flour or corn tortillas, place between pieces of moist paper toweling. When heating for enchiladas and other sauce-covered tortilla meals, dip in the heated sauces. You are covering two tasks at one time, making them more flexible for rolling and coating with sauce.

SALMON CHOWDER

Watch for sales on salmon at your grocery store. This is really an inexpensive and QUICK soup to prepare at the last minute.

1/2 cup celery, chopped
1/2 cup green pepper, chopped
1 small onion, chopped
1 clove garlic, finely minced
3 tablespoons butter
1 14-ounce can chicken broth
1 large potato, peeled and diced
1 cup carrots, shredded
1 teaspoon salt
1/2 teaspoon pepper
3/4 teaspoon dill weed
1 10-ounce salmon filet
1 tablespoon olive oil
1 tablespoon lemon juice
1 14-ounce can cream-style corn
2 cups milk or 12-ounce can evaporated
    milk plus 1/2 cup water

In large pan, sauté celery, green pepper, onion and garlic in butter 5 minutes. Add broth, potato, carrots, salt, pepper and dill weed. Bring to boil. Reduce heat. Cover and simmer 40 minutes. While soup is simmering, cook salmon. In small skillet, sauté salmon in olive oil and lemon juice. Flake and add to soup. Add corn and milk. Heat through, but do not boil. Ladle into soup bowls and garnish with sprinkle of dill weed. Serves 8.

Per serving: 203 calories; 10.0 fat grams

Frozen seafood can be defrosted by immersing in cold water for up to an hour. The longer seafood cooks the tougher and drier it becomes and the flavor fades. When done, fish flakes easily at the touch of a fork.

CREAMY CHINESE CHICKEN SOUP

The hardest thing about preparing this soup is opening the cans. You don't even have to thaw the vegetables.

2 cups cooked chicken, shredded
1 onion, chopped
2 cloves garlic, minced
1 16-ounce package frozen Chinese
    vegetables
1 10-ounce can cream of mushroom soup
1 10-ounce can cream of chicken soup
1 10-ounce can chicken broth
2 cups water
1/4 cup instant rice
1 tablespoon soy sauce

In large sprayed pan, sauté chicken, onion and garlic 5 minutes. Add remaining ingredients. Mix well. Bring to boil; reduce heat and simmer 30 minutes. Do not allow to boil. Serves 8.

Per serving: 160 calories; 4.6 fat grams

Buy egg rolls from your favorite Chinese restaurant to offer as a side to this soup (Yea Cyndis!!). Crisp 5 minutes in 350° oven.

Notes:

Miscellaneous

WATERMELON SLUSH

Welcome family and friends to a delicious meal by offering this refreshing starter. Make watermelon cubes ahead so there is very little last minute preparation.

3 1/2 pounds seedless watermelon
3/4 cup pineapple juice or white grape juice
1/2 cup rum, optional, or more fruit juice
1/3 cup lemon juice
Sugar, if needed, to taste

Cut rind off watermelon; discard. Cut fruit into 1/2-inch chunks. Line 10 x 15-inch pan with plastic wrap. Arrange fruit on wrap in a single layer. Freeze 1-2 hours until firm. (If making ahead or making several batches, transfer frozen chunks to freezer bag and repeat). In blender, combine combine half the pineapple juice, rum and lemon juice. Whirl, gradually dropping in half the frozen watermelon chunks, until smoothly puréed. Sweeten to taste with sugar. Pour into a pitcher or directly into glasses. Repeat to make second batch. Keep slushy by storing in freezer while finishing first batch. Serves 6-8.

Per serving: 81 calories; 0.5 fat grams

 Serve this slush as a light dessert by scooping into halved hollowed out lemon rinds. Keep whole units frozen firmly. Serve in center of small bowls or plates surrounded with frozen blackberries or other fresh fruit.

RASPBERRY TEA

Georgie created a similar iced tea for a signing we hosted. Serve it hot on a cold winter day.

2 cups brewed raspberry tea
2 cups cranberry-raspberry juice
1 cup prepared lemonade
1/4 cup water
Sugar, optional
1 lemon, thinly sliced
Fresh or frozen raspberries, optional

In large pitcher, combine tea, juice, lemonade and water. Taste to determine the need for sugar; add, if necessary. Moisten rims of champagne or small margarita glasses with lemon slice. Dip in sugar. Add ice. Pour tea into glasses and float lemon slices on top. Drop 2-3 raspberries in glasses (will sink to bottom). Serves 6.

Per serving: 95 calories; 0.1 fat grams

To serve tea hot, mash 1 cup fresh or frozen raspberries in large pan. Add tea, juice, lemonade, water and 3 whole allspice. Bring to boil; reduce heat. Simmer, uncovered, 10 minutes. Strain into heated carafe or another pan; discard fruit pulp and spices. Ladle into mugs. Float lemon slices and drop in 3-4 raspberries.

IRISH COFFEE

This San Franciscan treat can be just enough 'dessert' after a great lunch. The Duncan family makes it a little lighter by using fat free half & half.

1 cup chilled heavy cream
8 teaspoons sugar
12 tablespoons Irish whiskey
4 cups strong hot coffee

In large mixer bowl, whip cream with sugar until it just holds stiff peaks. Pour 3 tablespoons Irish whiskey into tall glass mugs. Add coffee to about 3/4-inch from top. Spoon whipped cream on top. Serves 4.

Per serving: 346 calories; 22.0 fat grams

Besides many flavored coffees available, liqueurs like Amaretto or Kahlua are delicious substitutions for Irish whiskey. Use flavored syrups for non-alcoholic coffee drinks.

FUZZY CHAMPAGNE

This is so easy and QUICK, but so elegant for a special Sunday brunch celebration.

4 peaches, skinned, pitted
3-4 teaspoons sugar
Piece of lime and sugar for rim of glass
1 bottle champagne or ginger ale

In blender purée peaches with sugar. Run piece of lime around 6 champagne glasses. Dip in sugar. Fill glass a little over half full with purée. Pour champagne or soda over purée. With small whisk, give a gentle spin to slightly mix. Serves 6.

Per serving: 168 calories; 0.0 fat grams

Use other seasonal fruits like strawberries, raspberries, blueberries, melons or mangos. The good taste never ends.

CRUNCHY GRANOLA

This granola is wonderful mixed into waffles or pancakes. It is good mixed with your favorite cereal, even oatmeal, and even more delicious mixed into yogurt. Keep it on your cupboard for a QUICK snack.

3 cups old-fashioned rolled oats
1/2 cup sliced almonds
1/2 cup wheat germ
1/2 cup whole wheat flour
1/4 cup oat bran
4 tablespoons brown sugar, packed
2 teaspoons cinnamon
Pinch of salt
1/2 teaspoon pumpkin pie spice
3/4 cup cranberry juice or unsweetened
     apple juice
4 tablespoons honey
1 tablespoon molasses
1 tablespoon vanilla
2 tablespoons butter, melted

Preheat oven to 300°. Spray large baking sheet. In large bowl, mix oats, almonds, wheat germ, flour, oat bran, brown sugar, cinnamon, salt and pumpkin pie spice. In 2-cup measuring cup, whisk together juice, honey, molasses, vanilla and butter. Pour over dry mixture, stirring to moisten all ingredients. Spread granola on baking sheet. Bake 45 minutes, stirring well every 15 minutes. Watch carefully so it doesn't burn; you may have to turn the oven to 250° or 275°. It will become crisp as it cools. Store in airtight container. Makes 6 cups (approximately 1/4 cup per serving).

Per serving: 108 calories; 3.5 fat grams

 Foot Note When measuring honey or molasses, first spray measuring cup so honey comes out easily. If honey crystallizes, remove lid and microwave 30 seconds; stir. Repeat until crystals dissolve.

HEALTHY GRANOLA BARS

These bars are soft with healthy ingredients for snacks or school lunches. They remind us of honey, butter and peanut butter sandwiches.

6 tablespoons butter, at room temperature
6 tablespoons honey
1/4 cup smooth peanut butter
2 tablespoons canola oil
1 cup rolled oats
3/4 cup whole wheat flour
1/2 cup wheat germ
1/2 cup pecans or walnuts, finely chopped
1/2 teaspoon baking powder
3/4 teaspoon cinnamon
1/4 teaspoon nutmeg

Preheat oven to 325°. Spray 10 x 13-inch baking pan. In large bowl, cream together butter, honey, peanut butter and oil until smooth. Stir in rest of ingredients. Press into baking pan with back of spoon that has been dipped in warm water. Bake 15 minutes or until the edges are browned. Cool and cut into bars. Makes 24 bars.

Per serving: 109 calories; 6.6 fat grams

Honey absorbs and retains moisture which prevents baked goods from drying out too quickly.

Honey has a higher sweetening power than sugar and is a natural source of energy.

Granola

HASH BROWN POTATO CASSEROLE

A holiday meal at the Patricks wouldn't be complete without "the potatoes", the Patrick name for this recipe. (Why have you not shared this with the Duncans until now, Georgie?)

2 12-ounce packages frozen hash browns
2 cups light sour cream
1 10-ounce can cream of chicken soup
1/2 cup butter or margarine, melted
1 teaspoon salt
1/2 teaspoon pepper
1 tablespoon minced onion
2 cups cheddar cheese, shredded
2 cups corn flakes, crushed
1/4 cup butter or margarine, melted

Preheat oven to 350°. Spray 9 x 13-inch baking dish. In large mixing bowl, combine first 8 ingredients. Mix well. Spread in baking dish. In medium bowl, toss corn flakes and 1/4 cup butter together. Sprinkle over top of casserole. Bake 30 minutes. Serves 12.

Per serving: 340 calories; 26.3 fat grams

Foot Notes

Make ahead and refrigerate. Pop in oven 50 minutes before serving.

Serve as a side to eggs, salads or sandwiches. Use any leftovers as a filler in homemade soup, like broccoli and cheese.

BREAKFAST POTATOES

Restaurants offer many potato varieties, each a specialty of that establishment. Hash browns are the favorite at the Duncan and Patrick establishments.

4 tablespoons oil, butter or combination of
    both
8-10 potatoes, cooked, peeled or unpeeled,
    cubed, sliced or shredded for hash
    browns
1/2 onion, finely chopped
1/2 cup green pepper, chopped
1 tablespoon pimiento or 2 tablespoons
    fresh red pepper, chopped
1 teaspoon chili powder
1/2 teaspoon cumin
1/2 teaspoon garlic salt
1/2 teaspoon pepper
1 tablespoon parsley

Heat oil in large skillet. Add potatoes, onion, green peppers and pimiento. Fry 10 minutes, turning often, until lightly browned on both sides. In small bowl, mix chili powder, cumin, garlic salt, pepper and parsley together. Sprinkle on potatoes and toss. Serve with eggs, sausage, ham or bacon. Serves 8-10.

Per serving: 106 calories; 5.6 fat grams

Boil several extra potatoes, refrigerate until cool and shred later. Divide into individual servings and put in freezer bags for a QUICK meal on another day.

POTATO PANCAKES

This is a QUICK version of a German favorite.

1 12-ounce package frozen hash brown
    potatoes, thawed
Bowl of ice cold water
1 onion, finely chopped
2 eggs, slightly beaten
1/2 cup sour cream
1/2 cup flour
1 teaspoon salt
Freshly ground pepper to taste
Pinch nutmeg
1/4 cup canola or peanut oil for frying

In large bowl of cold water, rinse hash browns. Drain well in colander (this is a very important step). Preheat oven to 200°. In clean bowl, thoroughly mix onion, eggs, sour cream, flour, salt, pepper and nutmeg with large spoon or hands. Meanwhile, heat oil to the point that a piece of potato dropped in oil sizzles immediately. With a large spoon, scoop a generous spoonful of potato mixture into oil. Flatten immediately. Turn over carefully with large, slotted spatula, browning both sides. Keep warm on paper towel lined baking sheet in oven. Serve while hot. Serves 4.

Per serving: 472 calories; 33.5 fat grams

Foot Notes

If serving later, set pancakes aside to cool to room temperature, refrigerate or freeze until ready to serve. Reheat pancakes in 350° oven.

When frying food, canola or peanut oil makes a crisper product and isn't absorbed as readily as other oil or butter.

POTATO AND ARTICHOKE PANCAKE

You need to work fast with this recipe, so have all ingredients ready.

4 large potatoes, cooked, peeled and
    coarsely shredded
3/4 teaspoon salt
1/4 teaspoon freshly ground pepper
2 tablespoons olive oil
1 cup mozzarella cheese
1 8-ounce jar marinated artichoke hearts,
    rinsed, well drained and sliced

Preheat oven to 400°. Place potatoes in large bowl. Pat dry. Toss with salt and pepper. In nonstick 10-inch skillet with heat-safe handle, heat 1 tablespoon olive oil over medium heat. Add half the potatoes, gently patting with rubber spatula or back of spoon to cover bottom of pan. Leaving 1/2-inch border, top potatoes with half the cheese, all the artichokes, then remaining cheese. Cover with remaining potatoes, patting to edge of pan. Cook 10 minutes, gently shaking pan to prevent sticking. Invert a large plate over skillet and carefully turn plate and skillet over so that pancake is now on plate. Add remaining tablespoon of oil to skillet, gently slide pancake back into skillet and cook 10 minutes longer again shaking to prevent sticking. Place skillet in oven. Bake, uncovered, 20 minutes. Serves 6.

Per serving: 163 calories; 9.3 fat grams

 Make this pancake QUICKer by using frozen, precooked hash browns.

COLD ASPARAGUS SIDE

This is a QUICK and tasty side dish or salad topper. It's way too simple.

12 fresh asparagus spears, partially cooked,
　　drained
1/2 cup zesty Italian salad dressing,
　　low calorie
Parmesan cheese

Place asparagus spears in 9 x 9-inch baking dish.
Cover with dressing and top with Parmesan cheese.
Refrigerate until ready to use. Serves 4.

Per serving: 79 calories; 4.6 fat grams

Cook asparagus in microwave by
placing asparagus spears in 9 x 9-inch
baking dish with 3-4 tablespoons
water. Cover with plastic wrap,
leaving one corner barely vented.
Cook on high 4 minutes. Drain. Cool
and follow recipe.

ASPARAGUS ROLLUPS

You have bread, veggie and meat all in one little package that can be served with many entrées.

12 slices high quality white bread, crusts
    removed
1 8-ounce container whipped cream cheese
2 tablespoons chives or green onions,
    chopped
8 slices bacon, cooked crisp, crumbled
24 fresh asparagus spears, partially cooked
3 tablespoons margarine or butter, melted
Parmesan cheese

Preheat oven to 400°. Spray large cookie sheet. Flatten each slice of bread with rolling pin. In small bowl, combine cream cheese, chives and bacon. Spread on bread covering to edges. Place 2 asparagus spears on each slice of bread. Roll up and place seam side down on cookie sheet. Brush each rollup with margarine; sprinkle with Parmesan cheese. Bake 10 minutes until lightly browned. Serves 12.

Per serving: 190 calories; 12.7 fat grams

 To make ahead, cover and refrigerate for up to 6 hours before baking.

BAKED CORN ON THE COB

Juicy fresh corn on the cob is the highlight of the summer.

1/2 cup butter or margarine, softened
2 tablespoons parsley or cilantro
2 tablespoons chives or green onions,
    chopped
1 teaspoon thyme or chili powder
1/2 teaspoon oregano
1/2 teaspoon salt
1/4 teaspoon cayenne pepper
8 ears fresh corn on the cob

Preheat oven to 400°. In large baking dish, combine all ingredients except corn. Melt in microwave 10 seconds. Place corn in butter mixture, turning to cover each side. Bake 10-15 minutes, turning once during baking. Serves 8.

Per serving: 147 calories; 12.0 fat grams

Wrap each butter covered ear in foil and grill or cook in the campfire. Prepare ahead, but cook 10-15 minutes before serving.

We pick up a lot of spice blends at trade shows and gourmet shops we attend. We have tried barbecue, cajun, Mexican and even Prairie Potato. They are all good sprinkled on corn dipped in butter and grilled in the husks.

BAKED TOMATOES

This is Cyndi's favorite way to use an abundance of garden tomatoes. They are so-o-o easy to fix and elegant as a side dish.

6 medium tomatoes, cut in half
1 tablespoon garlic salt
1/2 cup Parmesan cheese
1/2 cup bread crumbs
Parsley

Preheat oven to 350°. Spray 9 x 13-inch baking dish. Place tomato halves in baking dish (may have to slice small sliver from bottom of tomato to get it to set evenly in dish). Sprinkle each with garlic salt, Parmesan cheese, bread crumbs and parsley. Bake 15-20 minutes until top is slightly browned. Serves 6.

Per serving: 91 calories; 3.0 fat grams

 This works just as well with drained canned tomatoes in the winter. Follow the same procedure. Save the juice from tomatoes for chili or other soups.

BAKED ZUCCHINI RINGS

This recipe was a 'what else can I do with this stuff' inspiration. It makes an attractive side to a salad and grilled chicken breast.

1 teaspoon chicken bouillon granules
1/4 cup water
6 center slices of an oversized zucchini,
    1 1/2-inches thick, seeded
2 tomatoes, chopped
2 green onions or 1/4 cup onion, finely
    chopped
1/2 cup broccoli, finely chopped
1/2 cup cucumber, finely chopped
1/4 cup black olives, finely chopped
1/2 cup Monterey Jack or white cheddar
    cheese, shredded
1/4 cup Parmesan cheese
2 tablespoons bread crumbs, optional

Preheat oven to 350°. Spray 10 x 15-inch baking dish. Combine bouillon and water in baking dish. Place zucchini rings in bouillon mixture. In large bowl, combine next 6 ingredients. Spoon into center of zucchini rings. Cover with foil. Bake 20 minutes. Remove cover and top with Parmesan cheese and bread crumbs. Bake 5 minutes longer. Serves 6.

Per serving: 95 calories; 4.9 fat grams

 The tomato mixture can be used in a smaller seeded zucchini and presented as a 'boat'. Increase baking time to 30 minutes.

BRUSHETTA-STYLE PORTABELLO MUSHROOMS

Georgie's son-in-law, Chad, a licensed chef, created this as a vegetarian main dish entrée for a bridge social. It is still getting rave reviews after 6 months, even from those of us who are not vegetarians.

4 portabello mushrooms
2 cloves garlic, minced
1/2 cup balsamic vinegar
1 teaspoon dry basil
1/4 teaspoon dry oregano
1/4 teaspoon dry thyme
1 cup olive oil
Salt and pepper to taste
3 tomatoes, diced
8 ounces basil pesto (found in the pasta section of grocery store)
1/2 cup mozzarella cheese, shredded (provolone or fresh mozzarella can be used)

Stem mushrooms and scrape the fan from under the cap using a spoon. Set aside. In small bowl, combine garlic, vinegar and herbs with whisk. Continue to whisk while slowly adding olive oil. Add salt and pepper. Place tomatoes in oil mixture; refrigerate at least 1 hour. Place mushroom caps on large baking sheet. Preheat oven to 350°. Spread 1/4 of pesto evenly on each mushroom cap. Spoon 2 tablespoons of tomato mixture on top of pesto. Top with cheese. Bake 10 minutes until cheese is melted and golden brown. To serve as side dish cut in fourths and arrange on plate with omelet, sandwich, salad or soup. Serves 8.

Per serving: 505 calories; 37.7 fat grams

Foot Note

The traditional Italian balsamic vinegar must be moved through a series of barrels made from a variety of woods for at least 12 years and up to 25 years. Commercial varieties may or may not be aged.

THIN MUD PIE SANDWICH

A tall, fat piece of Mud Pie is just too much for a lunch dessert. But, often guests still need a small piece of something sweet to get on with our day. Try this QUICK version.

1 16-ounce package chocolate cookie
    crumbs
1/2 cup butter or margarine, melted
1/2 gallon coffee-flavored ice cream (can use
    mint, cookies and cream or any flavor
    you like), softened at room temperature
1 10-ounce jar chocolate-fudge ice cream
    topping
1/2 cup walnuts, chopped, optional

In large bowl, mix cookie crumbs with butter. Press half into 9 x 13-inch baking dish. Cool while softening ice cream. Spoon ice cream over cookie crumbs, spreading gently with warm spoon. Cover with remainder of cookie crumbs. Freeze until firm. When ready to serve cut into squares. Drizzle plate with chocolate fudge topping, place an ice cream square on top, drizzle with fudge topping and sprinkle with nuts ("and a ton of whipped cream," Georgie says). Garnish with maraschino cherry, fresh strawberry or fresh raspberries. Serves 12.

Per serving: 489 calories; 25.8 fat grams

Foot Note

Chocolate Mousse Freeze
Follow directions without using the butter in the cookie crumbs. Mix a chocolate mousse-type instant pudding according to directions. Can be assembled in pie plates and served as a pie. For a nice presentation, assemble in a springform pan and serve from a pedestal plate.

BETTER THAN SEX CAKE

What else is there to say!! Serve for lunch and plan to take the rest of the day off (what won't our Nebraska friends think of. . .).

1 package chocolate cake, prepared according to directions in 9 x 13-inch baking dish
1 14-ounce can sweetened condensed milk
1 10-ounce jar caramel sauce
1 12-ounce carton frozen whipped topping, thawed
1 12-ounce package butter brickle bits

Poke holes into cake with handle of wooden spoon. Pour and spread condensed milk and caramel sauce on top while cake is still warm. Refrigerate. When ready to serve, cover with whipped topping and butter brickle bits. Serves 12.

Per serving: 690 calories; 36.3 fat grams

 Foot Note
Variations to this delicious dessert:

1. Drizzle cake with Amaretto and spread with pudding mixture, whipped topping and butter brickle bits.
2. Drizzle cake with raspberry sauce, whipped topping and fresh raspberries.

DESSERT CREPES

We want to show the versatility of crepes. We have given you great entrée crepes and now we add crepes for dessert. Follow the basic recipe for crepes on page 26.

Creme de Cacao Crepes

1 8-ounce package cream cheese
1 cup powdered sugar
1/2 cup creme de cacao liqueur
1 cup whipping cream
1 cup chocolate sauce
1/2 cup walnuts, chopped
12 dessert crepes

Flaming Cherry Crepes

1 cup light sour cream
1/3 cup brown sugar, packed
1 21-ounce can cherry pie filling
1 teaspoon orange extract
8 dessert crepes

Strawberry Preserve Crepes

1/2 cup whipping cream
1/2 cup light sour cream
2 tablespoons powdered sugar
1/4 teaspoon nutmeg
1 cup strawberry preserves
8 dessert crepes

Creme de Cacao Crepes

In mixing bowl, whip cream cheese and powdered sugar until fluffy. Stir in liqueur. In large bowl, whip cream into peaks. Fold into cream cheese mixture. Fill crepe with 3 tablespoons filling. Roll. Top with chocolate sauce and walnuts. Serves 12.
Per serving: 333 calories; 18.1 fat grams

Flaming Cherry Crepes

Preheat oven to 350°. In small bowl, blend sour cream and brown sugar. Spread 2-3 tablespoon mixture down center of crepe. Roll; place seam down on ovenproof platter. Bake 5 minutes. Heat cherry filling in covered bowl in microwave 1 minute. Stir and spoon over crepes. Pour extract on pie filling. Ignite and serve immediately. Serves 8.
Per serving: 183 calories; 3.9 fat grams

Strawberry Preserve Crepes

In mixer bowl, beat cream, sour cream, powdered sugar and nutmeg. Spread crepe with 1 tablespoon filling; spoon 1 tablespoon strawberry preserves over filling. Roll crepes; place seam side down on serving plate. Sprinkle with powdered sugar and garnish with strawberries. Serves 8.
Per serving: 225 calories; 9.1 fat grams

CRANBERRY PECAN PIE

Our friend Mar says, "This is so easy that even I can do it!" She claims to be a noncook but always feeds us well when we visit.

1 cup fresh cranberries
1 unbaked pie crust
1/2 cup pecans
1/2 cup sugar
1 egg
1/2 cup sugar
1/2 cup flour
1/4 cup butter or margarine, melted
2 tablespoons shortening, melted

Preheat oven to 350°. Wash cranberries; drain. Place in pie crust. Spread pecans and 1/2 cup sugar over cranberries. In medium bowl, beat egg; add 1/2 cup sugar and mix well. Beat in flour, butter and shortening. Pour batter over cranberries. Bake 45 minutes. Serve with scoop of ice cream. Serves 8.

Per serving: 341 calories; 18.0 fat grams

 Did you know that cranberries bounce? The good ones really bounce and are called 'bouncing berries'; the bad ones stick to the surface.

PUMPKIN PIE CAKE

Mar first served this at a family birthday. She admits that, "Sometimes this is soupier than other times but always good!"

1 29-ounce can pumpkin
1 13-ounce can light evaporated milk
3 eggs
1 teaspoon nutmeg
1/2 teaspoon ginger
1/2 teaspoon ground cloves
1/2 teaspoon salt
2 teaspoons cinnamon
1 1/2 cups sugar
1 box yellow cake mix
1 cup walnuts, chopped
1 cup butter or margarine, melted

Preheat oven to 350°. Spray 9 x 13-inch baking dish. In large bowl, beat pumpkin, milk, eggs, spices and sugar well. Pour into baking dish. Sprinkle cake mix over pumpkin mixture. Gently pat down with spoon. Sprinkle with walnuts. Drizzle butter over cake mix. Bake 50 minutes. Cool and cut into squares. Garnish with dollop of whipped cream. Serves 12.

Per serving: 498 calories; 23.0 fat grams

 Try gingerbread mix in place of the yellow cake mix. It's a surprisingly good combination with pumpkin.

RASPBERRY CREAM PARFAITS

A gorgeous, light and creamy dessert.

1 cup boiling water
1 3-ounce package raspberry flavored
  gelatin
1/2 pint vanilla ice cream
2 10-ounce packages frozen raspberries,
  partially thawed

In medium bowl, pour boiling water over gelatin, stirring until gelatin is dissolved. Stir in ice cream and 1 package raspberries. Chill 15 minutes until partially set. In blender, purée last package raspberries. Reserve 1/2 cup. Divide purée among 8 parfait glasses. Spoon raspberry cream mixture into glasses over purée. Spoon reserved purée on top. Refrigerate. Serve with a delicate cookie. Serves 8.

Per serving: 147 calories; 1.9 fat grams

Melba Dessert

Dissolve 1 3-ounce package peach flavored gelatin in 1 cup boiling water. Stir in 1 10-ounce package frozen peaches and 1/2 pint ice cream. Chill. Purée 1 10-ounce package frozen raspberries, partially thawed. Save 1/2 cup. Divide raspberry purée among 8 parfait glasses. Spoon peach cream mixture into glasses. Top with reserved raspberry purée.

Desserts

OUTSIDE-INSIDE GERMAN CHOCOLATE CAKE

This is very rich and moist and gets better with age.

1 box German chocolate cake mix
2 16-ounce cans coconut pecan frosting
Fudge topping, optional

Preheat oven to 350°. Spray bundt pan generously. Coat with sugar. Mix cake according to directions on package. Stir in 1 can of frosting. Pour batter into pan. Bake 50-55 minutes. Cool completely. Spread last can of frosting on top. To serve, drizzle warm fudge topping on plate before placing slice of cake on it. Serves 16.

Per serving: 342 calories; 18.7 fat grams

 Chocolate fudge frosting can be substituted for the last can of coconut pecan frosting. Use half can to spread on cake and heat second half in microwave to drizzle on the plate.

CARAMEL PEAR MUFFIN

Oh, my! The cheeks just clinch thinking about how good this is.

3 tablespoons light cream cheese, softened
3 English muffins, split
1 15-ounce can chunky pears, drained
1/4 teaspoon cinnamon
1/2 cup caramel sauce
1/4 cup butter brickle bits (found in the
    chocolate chip section of grocery store)
2 tablespoons pecans, finely chopped
1 1/2 pints light vanilla ice cream

Preheat oven to 375°. Spray baking pan. Spread cream cheese evenly on each muffin half. In small bowl, toss pears with cinnamon and 1/4 cup caramel sauce. Arrange pear mixture on cream cheese. Bake 10-15 minutes. Carefully remove muffins to serving plates. Cool 5 minutes. Top muffins with toffee bits, pecans and scoop of ice cream. Drizzle 1/4 cup caramel over all, if desired. Serve immediately. Serves 6.

Per serving: 307 calories; 10.1 fat grams

 To toast nuts, heat in sprayed skillet until slightly browned, stirring to prevent burning. Sliced almonds start toasting right away, so watch carefully. Use the same method for toasting sesame seeds.

BERRY TRIFLE

Use any kind of berry in this recipe or mix them for variety. It is an impressive ending to a meal.

1 16-ounce light pound cake, cut into 18 slices, or 2 3-ounce packages ladyfingers

2 3-ounce packages instant vanilla pudding mix

1 18-ounce jar raspberry, strawberry or choice jam

1 1/2 pints fresh fruit of choice, 6 pieces reserved

1/2 cup whipped topping

Arrange 6 cake slices on bottom of trifle dish or large decorative bowl. Prepare pudding according to directions on package. Place 6 cake slices evenly around outside of bowl, using half of pudding to hold them in place. Gently combine jam and fruit. Spoon half over pudding. Layer remaining cake, pudding and fruit mixture. Chill. Garnish with whipped topping and reserved fruit. Refrigerate. Serves 12.

Per serving: 367 calories; 9.4 fat grams

 A garnish of **Toasted Coconut Bananas** would top this treat off just right:

Slice bananas crosswise in 1-inch pieces. Roll in orange juice to keep from browning, then in toasted coconut. To toast coconut, spread in pie plate and heat in 350° oven stirring often until browned.

WHITE BROWNIES

This section wouldn't be complete without a brownie recipe. This one is a diversion from the regular chocolate brownie and compliments fruit well. It also satisfies Cyndi's urge to "drizzle".

2 eggs
1 cup sugar
1/2 cup butter or margarine, softened
1 cup flour
Pinch of salt
2 teaspoons almond extract
1/2 16-ounce can vanilla frosting
1/4 cup pecans, chopped

Preheat oven to 350°. Spray 9 x 9-inch baking dish. In mixer bowl, beat eggs, sugar, butter, flour, salt and 1 teaspoon almond extract 1 minute. Scrape edges and mix well. Spread in baking dish. Bake 25-30 minutes. Cool. Mix 1 teaspoon almond extract with frosting. Spread on brownies while slightly warm. (To drizzle frosting, thin with a little water or milk.) Sprinkle with pecans. Cut into squares. Serves 9-12.

Per serving: 280 calories; 12.4 fat grams

Foot Note
Refrigerate brownies between layers of waxed paper or parchment paper in airtight container for up to 2 weeks. Brownies freeze well.

Desserts

Notes:

Index

Breads

Angel Buns, 16
Apricot Bread, 6
Blueberry Crumb Muffins, 19
Breadsticks, 20
Caraway Puffs, 5
Cheddar Cheese Biscuits, 3
Cornmeal Streusel Coffee Cake, 14
Cranberry Bread, 7
Danish Bars, 2
Dill and Parmesan Rolls, 4
Dilly Bread, 21
French Cheese Bread, 22
Georgie's Monkey Bread, 15
German Donuts, 17
Lemon Bread, 9
Pineapple Zucchini Bread, 12
Poppy Seed Bread, 10
Pumpkin Bread, 11
Rhubarb-Orange Muffins, 18
Spiced Pecan Coffee Cake, 13
Sweet Poppy Seed Bread, 8
Tomato-Basil Focaccia, 23

Brunches

Artichoke and Spinach Crepes, 29
Asparagus Quiche, 45
Bacon and Mushroom Quiche, 41
Bacon and Swiss Brunch Pie, 58
Baked Blintzes, 33
Basic Crepes, 26
Basic Omelet, 34
Blueberry French Toast, 71
Breakfast Pizza, 49
Buttermilk Biscuits and Sausage Gravy, 63
Chicken Divan Crepes, 27
Crab Bake, 51
Crab Quiche, 44
Deviled Eggs in Cheese Sauce, 56
Egg & Sausage Quiche, 38
Eggs Benedict, 62
Fruit Sauce, 64
Granola Pancakes, 66
Ham and Vegetable Quiche, 39
Ham and Cheese Crepes, 32
Hash Brown and Egg Skillet, 54
Heidi's Breakfast Casserole, 50
Huevos Rancheros, 60
Italian Harvest Omelet, 37
Layered Breakfast, 48
Lowfat French Toast, 68
Meatless Breakfast Burritos, 59
Mexican Strata, 52
Mushroom Crust Quiche, 42
Oatmeal Wheat Waffles, 67
Overnight Artichoke Bake, 53
Pecan Crusted Chicken Quiche, 47
Peek-A-Boo Toast, 65
Sallie's Egg Casserole, 57

Index

Salmon Omelet with Cucumber Sauce, 36
Scrambled Egg Casserole, 55
Seafood Crepes, 31
Shrimp Quiche, 43
Spinach and Tomato Salsa Omelet, 35
Spinach Crepes, 30
Spinach Pie, 46
Stuffed French Toast, 69
Swiss Quiche, 40
Texas French Toast, 70
Turkey and Cranberry Crepes, 28
Vegetable Hash, 61

Lunches

Asparagus Ham Sandwiches, 75
Baked Ham & Swiss Sandwiches, 74
Barbecue Burgers and Salsa, 82
Black Bean Tortilla Pie, 98
Butter Bean Soup, 119
Chicken Caesar Wrap, 94
Chicken Crescent Squares, 88
Chicken or Turkey Casserole, 102
Chicken Quesadillas, 89
Creamy Chicken Breasts, 104
Creamy Chinese Chicken Soup, 125
Crispy Salmon Fillets, 108
Croissant Chicken Salad Sandwich, 85
Curried Beef Pitas, 83
Fajita Casserole, 99
Fresh Veggie Pasta, 110

Great Northern Minestrone, 122
Ham and Swiss Tortilla Wrap, 91
Hot Chicken Salad, 113
Hot Crab Boats, 106
Hot Ham Hoagies, 76
Hot Leftover Pasta Salad Plus, 111
Maple Chicken Salad, 112
Meatball Sandwiches, 79
Meatball Soup, 121
Mexican Chicken, 100
Mexican Pork Stew, 120
Mini Pizzas, 95
Not Too Spicy Gazpacho, 118
Open Face Reubens, 87
Open Face Tuna Melt, 86
Pasta Crusted Beef Pie, 103
Patrick Deli Hoagies, 77
Picnic Lunch in a Foil Packet, 109
Pizza Burgers, 80
Salmon Cakes, 107
Salmon Chowder, 124
Shish Kabobs with Georgie's Marinade, 96
Shrimp Scampi Kabobs, 97
Shrimp Stuffed Potatoes, 105
Sloppy Joes, 81
Strawberry Spinach Toss, 116
Sweet and Sour Spinach Salad, 115
Swiss and Spinach Calzone, 90
Tomato and Fresh Mozzarella Salad, 117
Tomato Basil Squares, 84

Tuna Burgers, 86
Tuna Salad with a Surprise, 114
Turkey on Spinach Wrap, 93
Veggies on Tomato Wrap, 92
Verde Bean Soup, 123
Western Turkey Casserole, 101
Zesty Italian Subs, 78

Miscellaneous

Beverages
Fuzzy Champagne, 131
Irish Coffee, 130
Raspberry Tea, 129
Watermelon Slush, 128

Desserts
Berry Trifle, 152
Better Than Sex Cake, 145
Caramel Pear Muffin, 151
Chocolate Mousse Freeze, 144
Cranberry Pecan Pie, 147
Creme de Cacao Crepes, 146
Dessert Crepes, 146
Flaming Cherry Crepes, 146
Melba Dessert, 149
Outside-Inside German Chocolate Cake, 150
Pumpkin Pie Cake, 148
Raspberry Cream Parfaits, 149
Strawberry Preserve Crepes, 146
Thin Mud Pie Sandwiches, 144

White Brownies, 153

Granola Treats
Crunchy Granola, 132
Healthy Granola Bars, 133

Side Dishes
Asparagus Rollups, 139
Baked Corn on the Cob, 140
Baked Tomatoes, 141
Baked Zucchini Rings, 142
Breakfast Potatoes, 135
Brushetta-Style Portabello Mushrooms, 143
Cold Asparagus Side, 138
Hash Brown Potato Casserole, 134
Potato and Artichoke Pancake, 137
Potato Pancakes, 136

Sauces, Spreads & Dressings

Barbecue Salsa, 82
Bearnaise Sauce, 30
Blueberry Sauce, 71
Cheese Sauce, 32, 57
Fresh Pico Salsa, 48
Hollandaise Sauce, 62
Horseradish Mayo, 77
Lemon-Honey Dressing, 116
Mock Caesar Salad Dressing, 94
Mock Hollandaise Sauce, 62
Sun-dried Tomato Dressing, 78
Sweet and Sour Dressing, 115

Index